BE STILL
DEVOTIONAL

PRAYER
JOURNAL
FOR

Eileen Nyberg

ADISAN Publishing AB

This Journal
Belongs To:

INTRODUCTION

I want you to be able to use this prayer journal to fill your heart with hope, optimism, and happiness every week throughout the year. This prayer journal can be used to strengthen your relationship with God throughout the year. This prayer journal can also help you get the guidance you need from God in every area of your life. I want you to feel happier and more at peace. You can also use this prayer journal to remind yourself who you are in Christ, what He is capable of doing in your life, and how having a personal relationship with Him can change your life in the best way possible.

How To Use This Book

This prayer journal can be used once a week to help give you hope and fill you with joy and optimism for each week ahead. You can read each devotional once a week for a year and grow in your faith. We want you to be encouraged and inspired by each devotional. After reading each devotional, you can look back at any time on the reflection points and see what you have learned throughout a year. You can also say prayers to strengthen your faith and grow in your relationship with God.

There are also places for coloring and shading Bible verses and journaling in each devotional. You can write and draw out your specific prayer requests and even mark when any of your prayers have been answered. You can even write out everything you are thankful for and what you hope will happen in your life. Through this devotional, you can fill your life with more hope, faith, and optimism to face each day with God at your side.

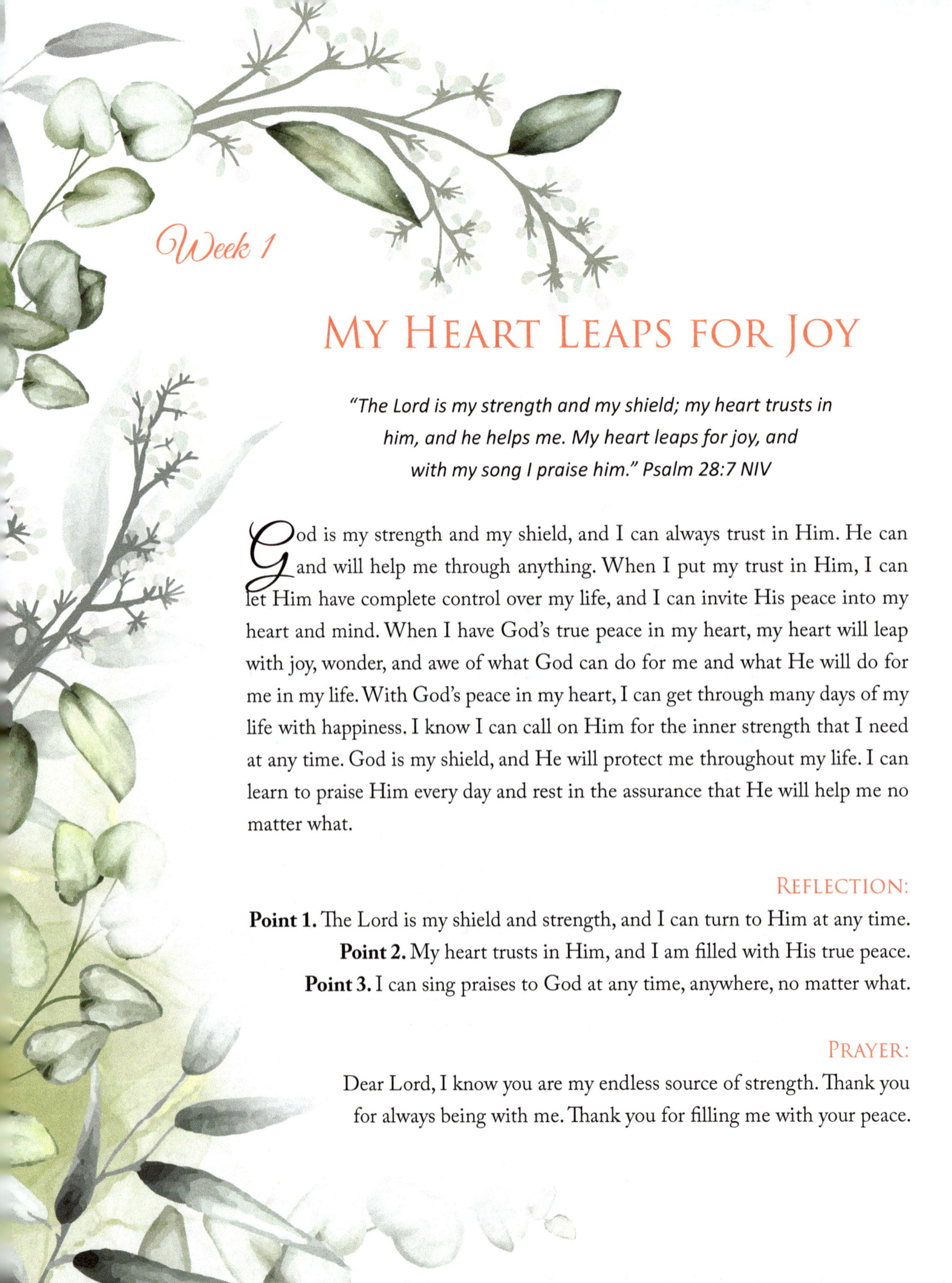

My Heart Leaps for Joy

"The Lord is my strength and my shield; my heart trusts in him, and he helps me. My heart leaps for joy, and with my song I praise him." Psalm 28:7 NIV

God is my strength and my shield, and I can always trust in Him. He can and will help me through anything. When I put my trust in Him, I can let Him have complete control over my life, and I can invite His peace into my heart and mind. When I have God's true peace in my heart, my heart will leap with joy, wonder, and awe of what God can do for me and what He will do for me in my life. With God's peace in my heart, I can get through many days of my life with happiness. I know I can call on Him for the inner strength that I need at any time. God is my shield, and He will protect me throughout my life. I can learn to praise Him every day and rest in the assurance that He will help me no matter what.

Reflection:

Point 1. The Lord is my shield and strength, and I can turn to Him at any time.

Point 2. My heart trusts in Him, and I am filled with His true peace.

Point 3. I can sing praises to God at any time, anywhere, no matter what.

Prayer:

Dear Lord, I know you are my endless source of strength. Thank you for always being with me. Thank you for filling me with your peace.

"....my God in whom I trust." Psalm 91:2

THINGS ON MY MIND

PRAYER REQUEST

PRAYERS ANSWERED

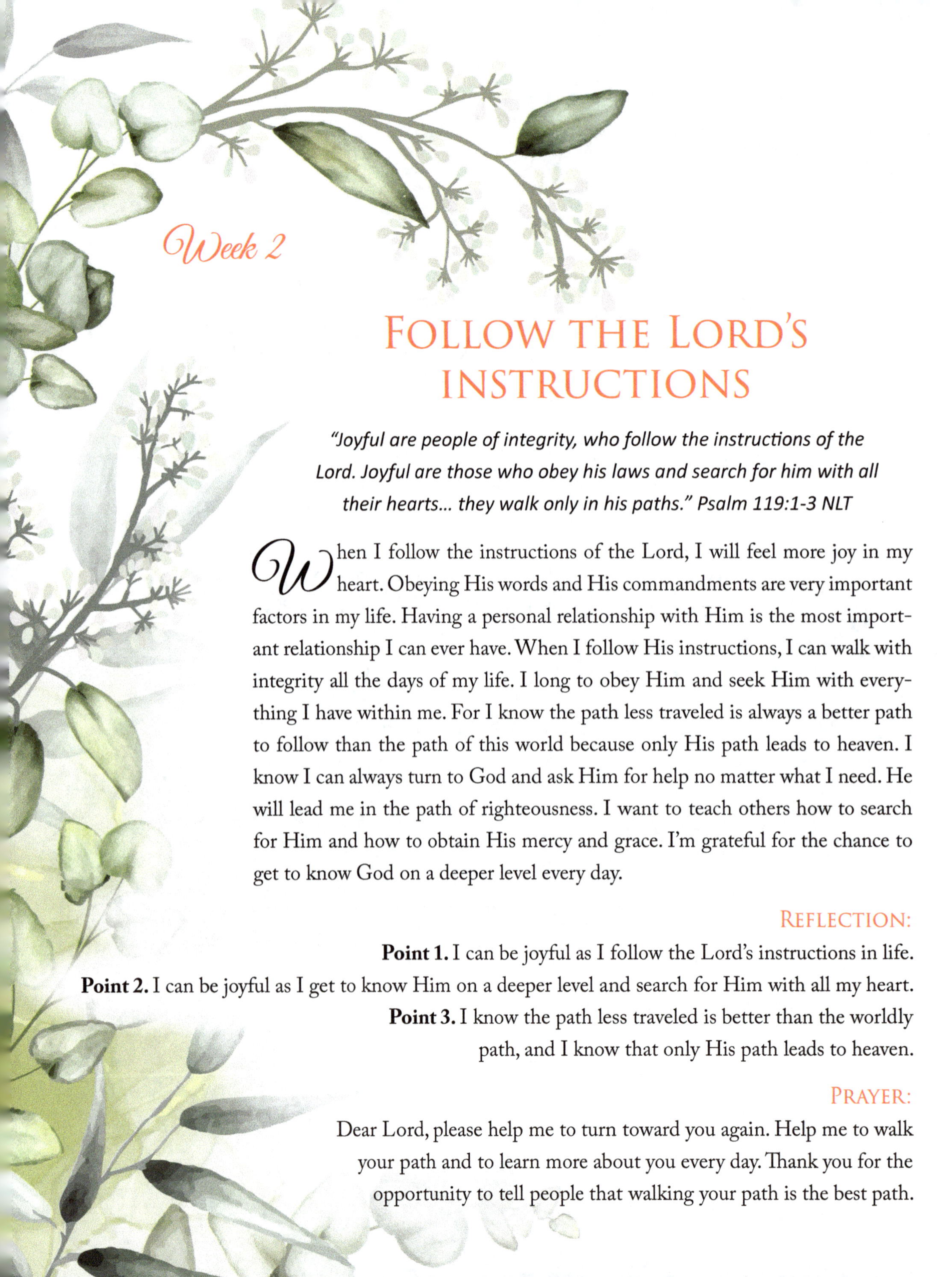

Follow the Lord's instructions

"Joyful are people of integrity, who follow the instructions of the Lord. Joyful are those who obey his laws and search for him with all their hearts… they walk only in his paths." Psalm 119:1-3 NLT

When I follow the instructions of the Lord, I will feel more joy in my heart. Obeying His words and His commandments are very important factors in my life. Having a personal relationship with Him is the most important relationship I can ever have. When I follow His instructions, I can walk with integrity all the days of my life. I long to obey Him and seek Him with everything I have within me. For I know the path less traveled is always a better path to follow than the path of this world because only His path leads to heaven. I know I can always turn to God and ask Him for help no matter what I need. He will lead me in the path of righteousness. I want to teach others how to search for Him and how to obtain His mercy and grace. I'm grateful for the chance to get to know God on a deeper level every day.

REFLECTION:

Point 1. I can be joyful as I follow the Lord's instructions in life.

Point 2. I can be joyful as I get to know Him on a deeper level and search for Him with all my heart.

Point 3. I know the path less traveled is better than the worldly path, and I know that only His path leads to heaven.

PRAYER:

Dear Lord, please help me to turn toward you again. Help me to walk your path and to learn more about you every day. Thank you for the opportunity to tell people that walking your path is the best path.

"Come near to God and he will come near to you." James 4:8

THINGS ON MY MIND

PRAYER REQUEST

PRAYERS ANSWERED

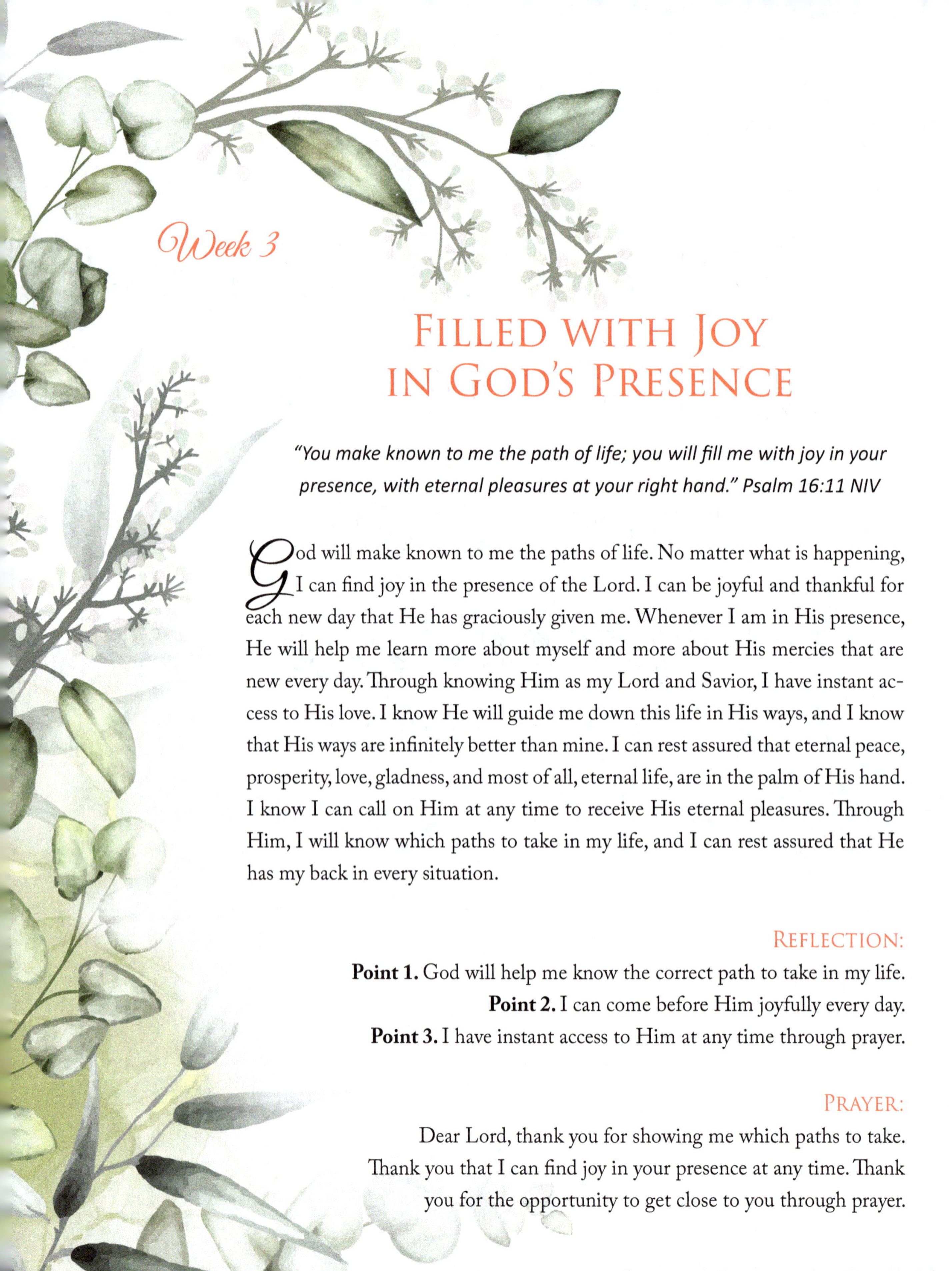

Filled with Joy in God's Presence

"You make known to me the path of life; you will fill me with joy in your presence, with eternal pleasures at your right hand." Psalm 16:11 NIV

God will make known to me the paths of life. No matter what is happening, I can find joy in the presence of the Lord. I can be joyful and thankful for each new day that He has graciously given me. Whenever I am in His presence, He will help me learn more about myself and more about His mercies that are new every day. Through knowing Him as my Lord and Savior, I have instant access to His love. I know He will guide me down this life in His ways, and I know that His ways are infinitely better than mine. I can rest assured that eternal peace, prosperity, love, gladness, and most of all, eternal life, are in the palm of His hand. I know I can call on Him at any time to receive His eternal pleasures. Through Him, I will know which paths to take in my life, and I can rest assured that He has my back in every situation.

Reflection:

Point 1. God will help me know the correct path to take in my life.

Point 2. I can come before Him joyfully every day.

Point 3. I have instant access to Him at any time through prayer.

Prayer:

Dear Lord, thank you for showing me which paths to take. Thank you that I can find joy in your presence at any time. Thank you for the opportunity to get close to you through prayer.

"...but rejoice that your names are written in heaven."
Luke 10:20

Things on My Mind

Prayer Request

Prayers Answered

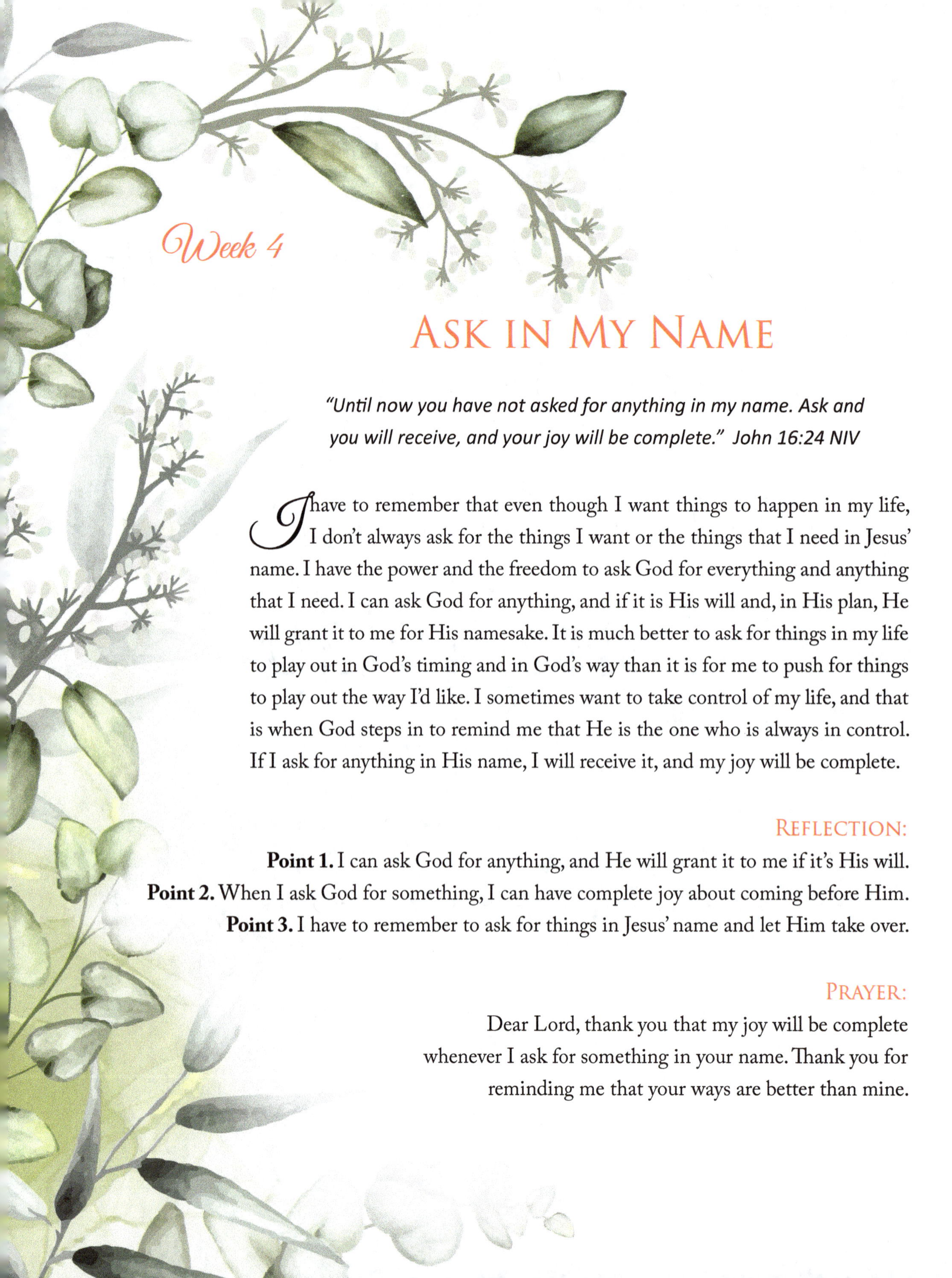

Ask in My Name

"Until now you have not asked for anything in my name. Ask and you will receive, and your joy will be complete." John 16:24 NIV

I have to remember that even though I want things to happen in my life, I don't always ask for the things I want or the things that I need in Jesus' name. I have the power and the freedom to ask God for everything and anything that I need. I can ask God for anything, and if it is His will and, in His plan, He will grant it to me for His namesake. It is much better to ask for things in my life to play out in God's timing and in God's way than it is for me to push for things to play out the way I'd like. I sometimes want to take control of my life, and that is when God steps in to remind me that He is the one who is always in control. If I ask for anything in His name, I will receive it, and my joy will be complete.

Reflection:

Point 1. I can ask God for anything, and He will grant it to me if it's His will.
Point 2. When I ask God for something, I can have complete joy about coming before Him.
Point 3. I have to remember to ask for things in Jesus' name and let Him take over.

Prayer:

Dear Lord, thank you that my joy will be complete whenever I ask for something in your name. Thank you for reminding me that your ways are better than mine.

"And my God will meet all your needs..." Philippians 4:19

THINGS ON MY MIND

PRAYER REQUEST

PRAYERS ANSWERED

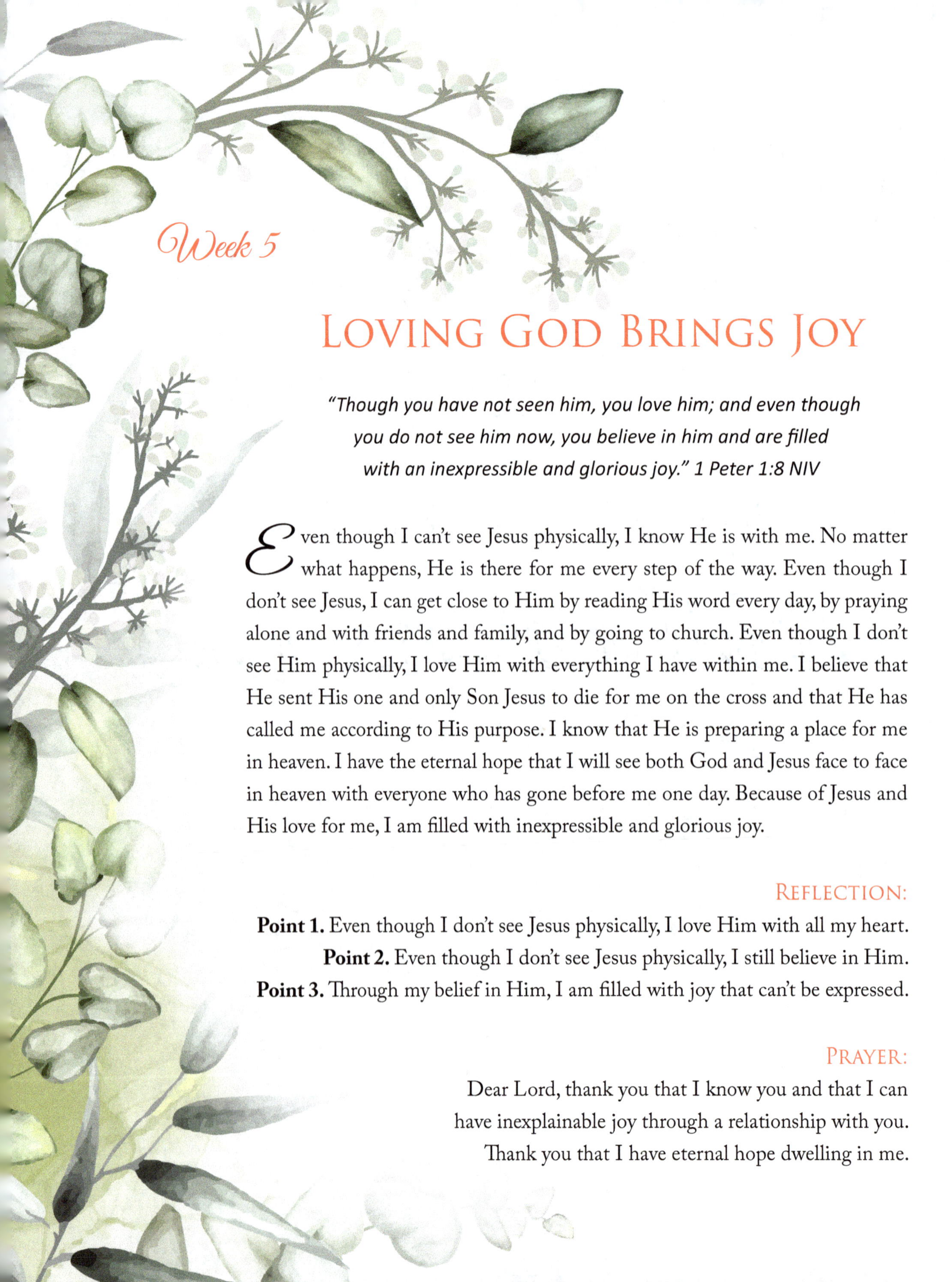

Loving God Brings Joy

"Though you have not seen him, you love him; and even though you do not see him now, you believe in him and are filled with an inexpressible and glorious joy." 1 Peter 1:8 NIV

Even though I can't see Jesus physically, I know He is with me. No matter what happens, He is there for me every step of the way. Even though I don't see Jesus, I can get close to Him by reading His word every day, by praying alone and with friends and family, and by going to church. Even though I don't see Him physically, I love Him with everything I have within me. I believe that He sent His one and only Son Jesus to die for me on the cross and that He has called me according to His purpose. I know that He is preparing a place for me in heaven. I have the eternal hope that I will see both God and Jesus face to face in heaven with everyone who has gone before me one day. Because of Jesus and His love for me, I am filled with inexpressible and glorious joy.

Reflection:

Point 1. Even though I don't see Jesus physically, I love Him with all my heart.
Point 2. Even though I don't see Jesus physically, I still believe in Him.
Point 3. Through my belief in Him, I am filled with joy that can't be expressed.

Prayer:

Dear Lord, thank you that I know you and that I can have inexplainable joy through a relationship with you. Thank you that I have eternal hope dwelling in me.

"Humble your- selves, therefore, under God's mighty hand..."

Things on My Mind

Prayer Request

Prayers Answered

Eat and Drink with Gladness

"Go, eat your food with gladness, and drink your wine with a joyful heart, for God has already approved what you do." Ecclesiastes 9:7 NIV

I can have happiness and joy all the days of my life, no matter what happens. I can be having dinner and be thankful that I have food to eat. Even if I don't always like the food, or it isn't my favorite, I can still find the joy to eat with my friends, kids, and family every night. I can sip my favorite drink and be grateful that I have beverages to drink. I can learn to be grateful for the things I have in my life, and I can count every moment that I get to eat or drink something as a blessing. No matter what happens, God says He already approves of what I'm doing in my life. I don't have to do anything to get Him to approve of me or my status. He already thinks of me as His beloved daughter. Nothing will ever change His mind about the way He thinks highly of me.

Reflection:

Point 1. I can eat my food and drink my drinks with happiness and joy every day.

Point 2. Nothing will ever change what God thinks of me.

Point 3. God thinks of me as His beloved daughter.

Prayer:

Dear Lord, please help me to remember that my food and drink are all gifts from you. Thank you for blessing me with food to eat and beverages to drink. Thank you that I am never in want.

1 Peter 5:6

"Give us today our daily bread."

Mathew 6:11

THINGS ON MY MIND

PRAYER REQUEST

PRAYERS ANSWERED

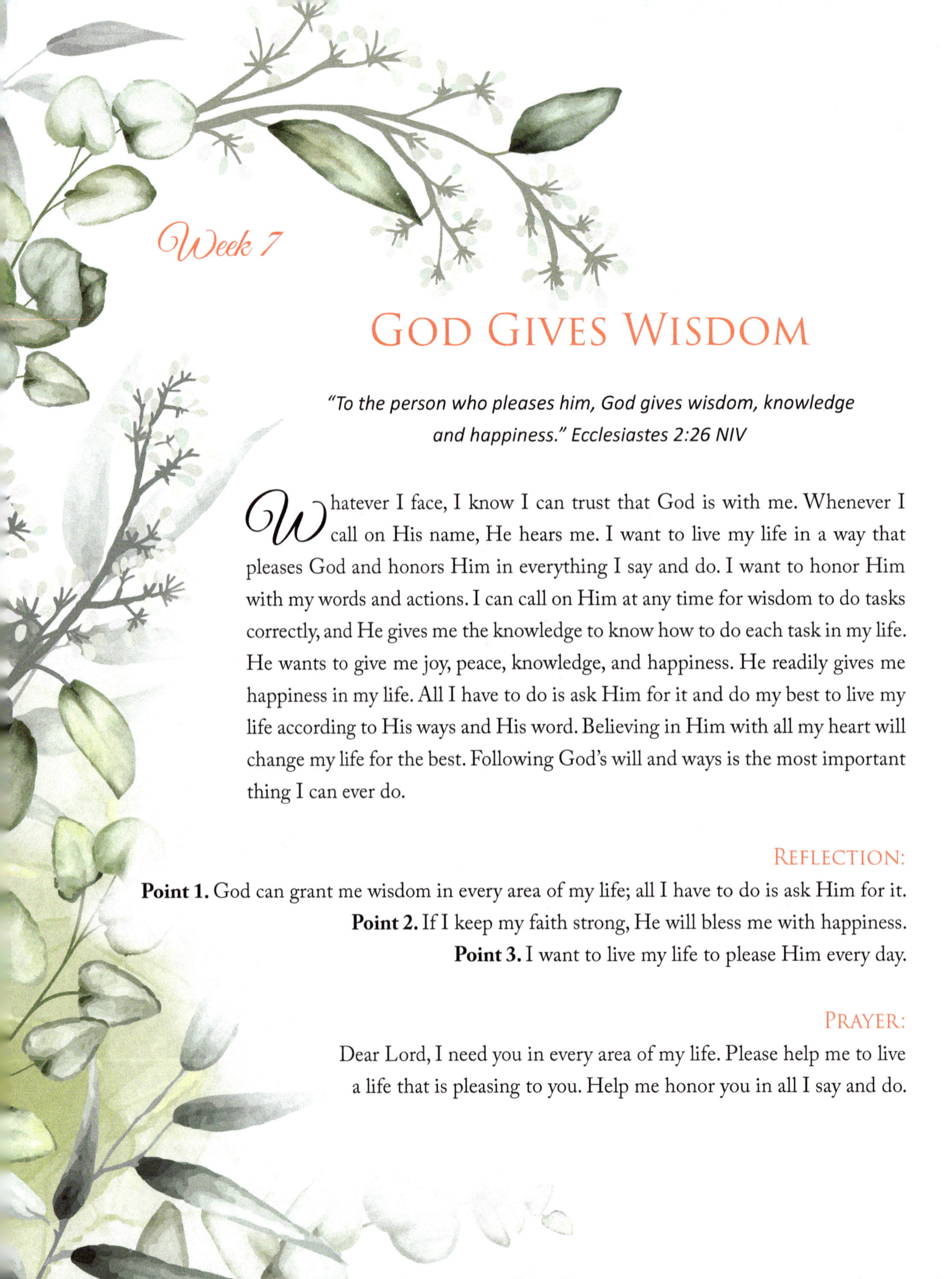

GOD GIVES WISDOM

"To the person who pleases him, God gives wisdom, knowledge and happiness." Ecclesiastes 2:26 NIV

Whatever I face, I know I can trust that God is with me. Whenever I call on His name, He hears me. I want to live my life in a way that pleases God and honors Him in everything I say and do. I want to honor Him with my words and actions. I can call on Him at any time for wisdom to do tasks correctly, and He gives me the knowledge to know how to do each task in my life. He wants to give me joy, peace, knowledge, and happiness. He readily gives me happiness in my life. All I have to do is ask Him for it and do my best to live my life according to His ways and His word. Believing in Him with all my heart will change my life for the best. Following God's will and ways is the most important thing I can ever do.

REFLECTION:

Point 1. God can grant me wisdom in every area of my life; all I have to do is ask Him for it.

Point 2. If I keep my faith strong, He will bless me with happiness.

Point 3. I want to live my life to please Him every day.

PRAYER:

Dear Lord, I need you in every area of my life. Please help me to live a life that is pleasing to you. Help me honor you in all I say and do.

"...from his mouth come knowledge and understanding." Proverbs 2:6

THINGS ON MY MIND

PRAYER REQUEST

PRAYERS ANSWERED

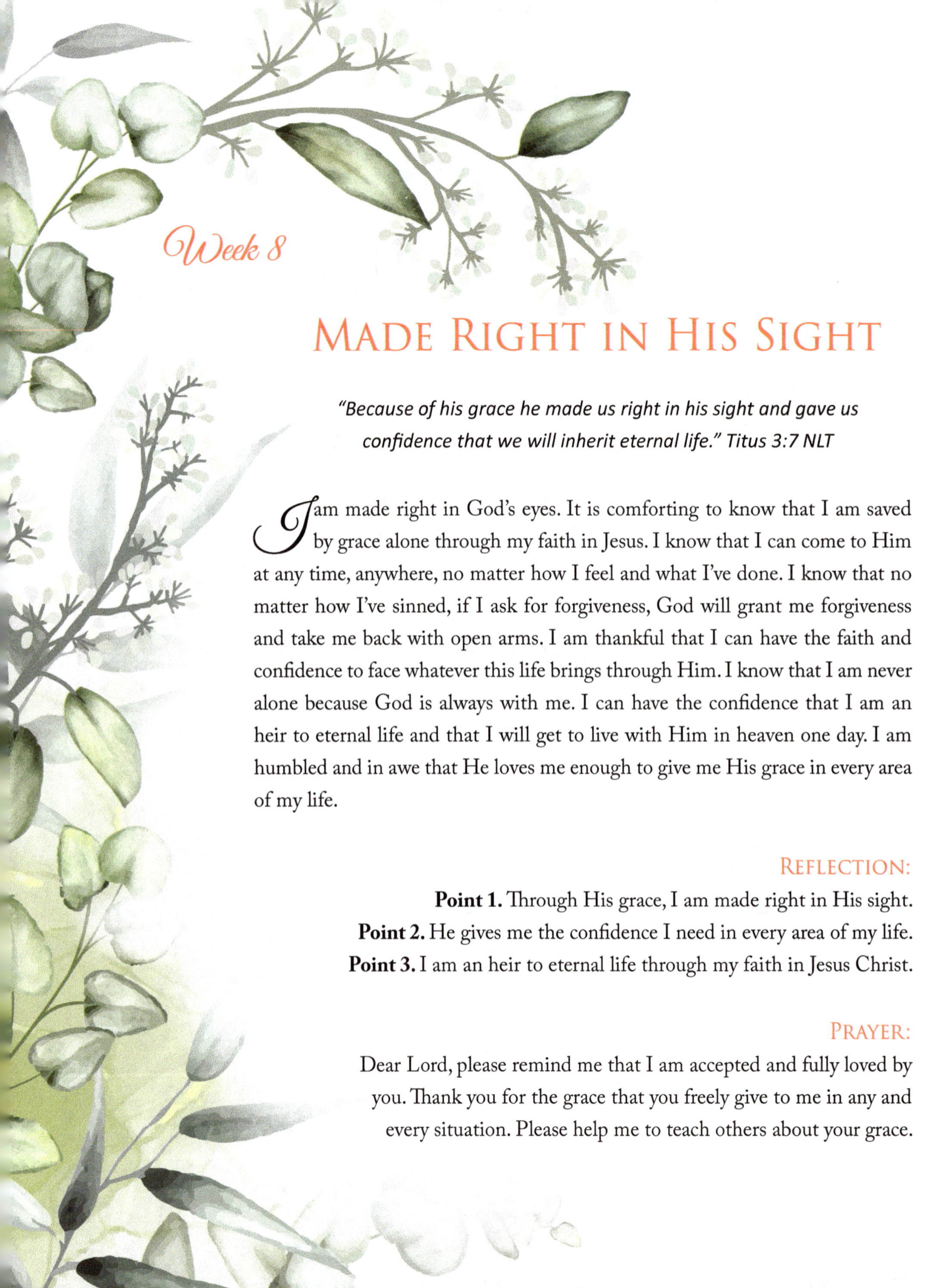

Made Right in His Sight

"Because of his grace he made us right in his sight and gave us confidence that we will inherit eternal life." Titus 3:7 NLT

I am made right in God's eyes. It is comforting to know that I am saved by grace alone through my faith in Jesus. I know that I can come to Him at any time, anywhere, no matter how I feel and what I've done. I know that no matter how I've sinned, if I ask for forgiveness, God will grant me forgiveness and take me back with open arms. I am thankful that I can have the faith and confidence to face whatever this life brings through Him. I know that I am never alone because God is always with me. I can have the confidence that I am an heir to eternal life and that I will get to live with Him in heaven one day. I am humbled and in awe that He loves me enough to give me His grace in every area of my life.

Reflection:

Point 1. Through His grace, I am made right in His sight.
Point 2. He gives me the confidence I need in every area of my life.
Point 3. I am an heir to eternal life through my faith in Jesus Christ.

Prayer:

Dear Lord, please remind me that I am accepted and fully loved by you. Thank you for the grace that you freely give to me in any and every situation. Please help me to teach others about your grace.

"God saved you by his grace when you believed." Ephesians 2:8

THINGS ON MY MIND

PRAYER REQUEST

PRAYERS ANSWERED

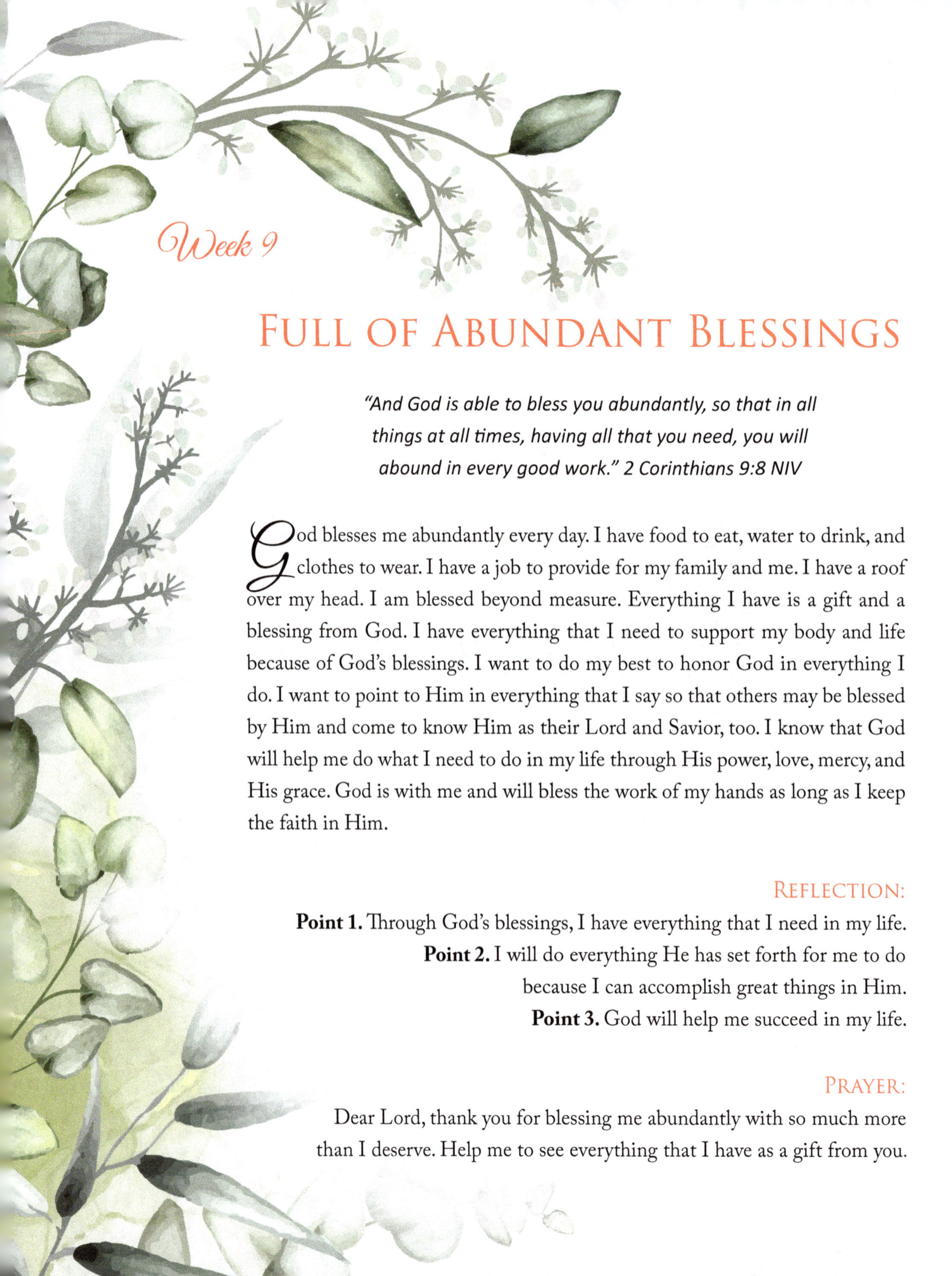

Full of Abundant Blessings

"And God is able to bless you abundantly, so that in all things at all times, having all that you need, you will abound in every good work." 2 Corinthians 9:8 NIV

God blesses me abundantly every day. I have food to eat, water to drink, and clothes to wear. I have a job to provide for my family and me. I have a roof over my head. I am blessed beyond measure. Everything I have is a gift and a blessing from God. I have everything that I need to support my body and life because of God's blessings. I want to do my best to honor God in everything I do. I want to point to Him in everything that I say so that others may be blessed by Him and come to know Him as their Lord and Savior, too. I know that God will help me do what I need to do in my life through His power, love, mercy, and His grace. God is with me and will bless the work of my hands as long as I keep the faith in Him.

Reflection:

Point 1. Through God's blessings, I have everything that I need in my life.
Point 2. I will do everything He has set forth for me to do because I can accomplish great things in Him.
Point 3. God will help me succeed in my life.

Prayer:

Dear Lord, thank you for blessing me abundantly with so much more than I deserve. Help me to see everything that I have as a gift from you.

"You know the generous grace of our Lord Jesus"
2 Corinthians 8-9

THINGS ON MY MIND

PRAYER REQUEST

PRAYERS ANSWERED

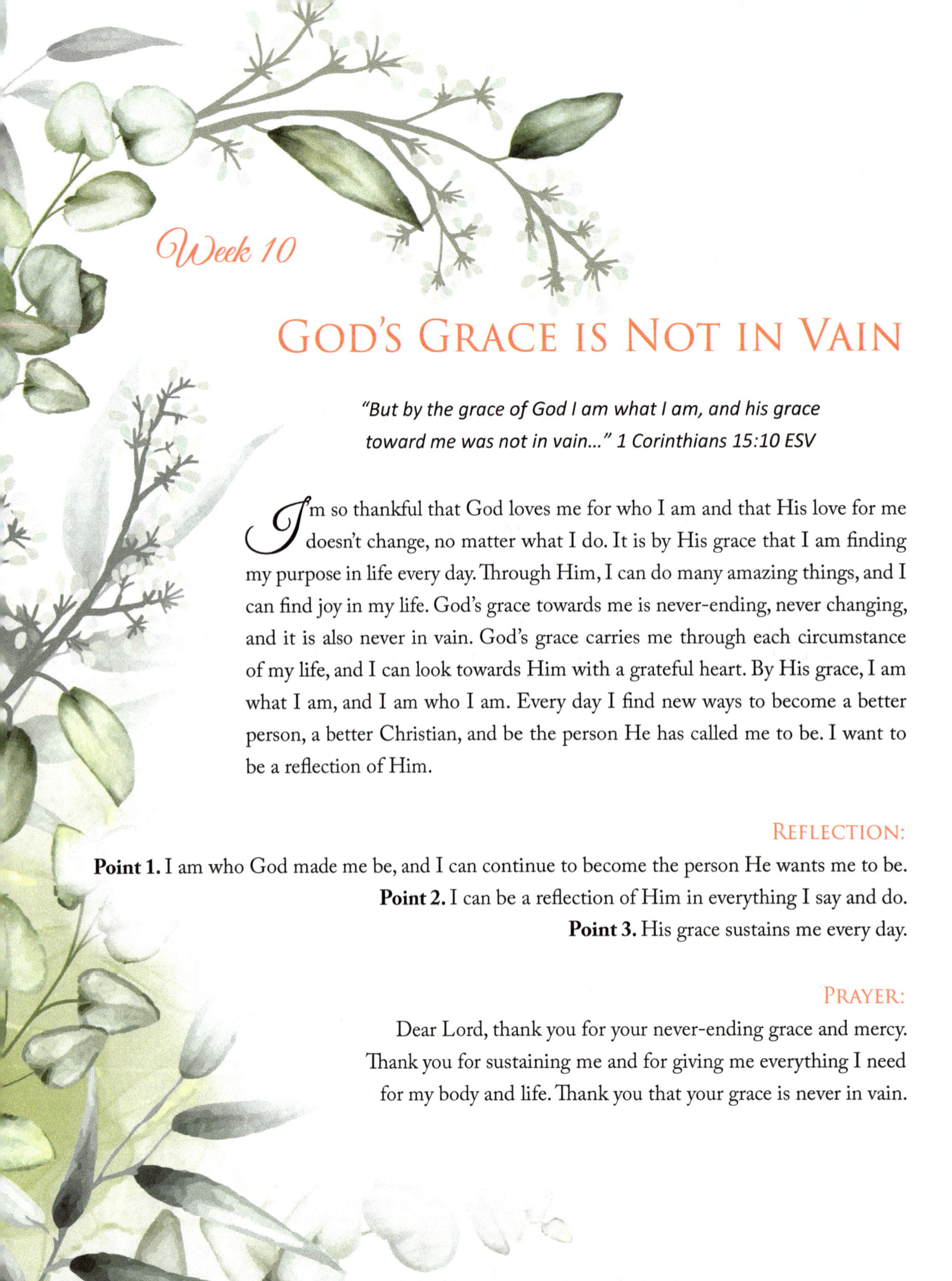

God's Grace is Not in Vain

"But by the grace of God I am what I am, and his grace toward me was not in vain…" 1 Corinthians 15:10 ESV

I'm so thankful that God loves me for who I am and that His love for me doesn't change, no matter what I do. It is by His grace that I am finding my purpose in life every day. Through Him, I can do many amazing things, and I can find joy in my life. God's grace towards me is never-ending, never changing, and it is also never in vain. God's grace carries me through each circumstance of my life, and I can look towards Him with a grateful heart. By His grace, I am what I am, and I am who I am. Every day I find new ways to become a better person, a better Christian, and be the person He has called me to be. I want to be a reflection of Him.

REFLECTION:

Point 1. I am who God made me be, and I can continue to become the person He wants me to be.

Point 2. I can be a reflection of Him in everything I say and do.

Point 3. His grace sustains me every day.

PRAYER:

Dear Lord, thank you for your never-ending grace and mercy. Thank you for sustaining me and for giving me everything I need for my body and life. Thank you that your grace is never in vain.

"My grace is sufficient for you."
2 Corinthians 12:9

THINGS ON MY MIND

PRAYER REQUEST   PRAYERS ANSWERED

Encourage Each Other

"So encourage each other and build each other up, just as you are already doing." 1 Thessalonians 5:11 NLT

I love it when my family and friends encourage me whenever I need it. I love it when God tells me that He is always there for me. Knowing that He is always there for me brings me so much peace. Having His peace in my heart allows me to think of how blessed I am to be able to turn to Him at any moment. It also allows me to see different ways that I can be an encouragement to my friends and family whenever they need a boost of faith. I can bring them one of their favorite meals or drinks and tell them that they are doing a great job at whatever task. I want to encourage them the way they encourage me. I want to be there for them in the same way that Jesus is there for me. I want to lift my family, friends, and co-workers in Jesus' name.

Reflection:

Point 1. I can be an encouragement to people the same way they encourage me.

Point 2. I can build people up just like God commands me to.

Point 3. I can have peace in my heart and bring His peace to others by just being kind to everyone around me.

Prayer:

Dear Lord, please help me to be an encourager to everyone I meet. Help me to build people up in the same way you build me up.

"...The pleasantness of a friend springs from their heartfelt advice." Proverbs 27:9

THINGS ON MY MIND

PRAYER REQUEST

PRAYERS ANSWERED

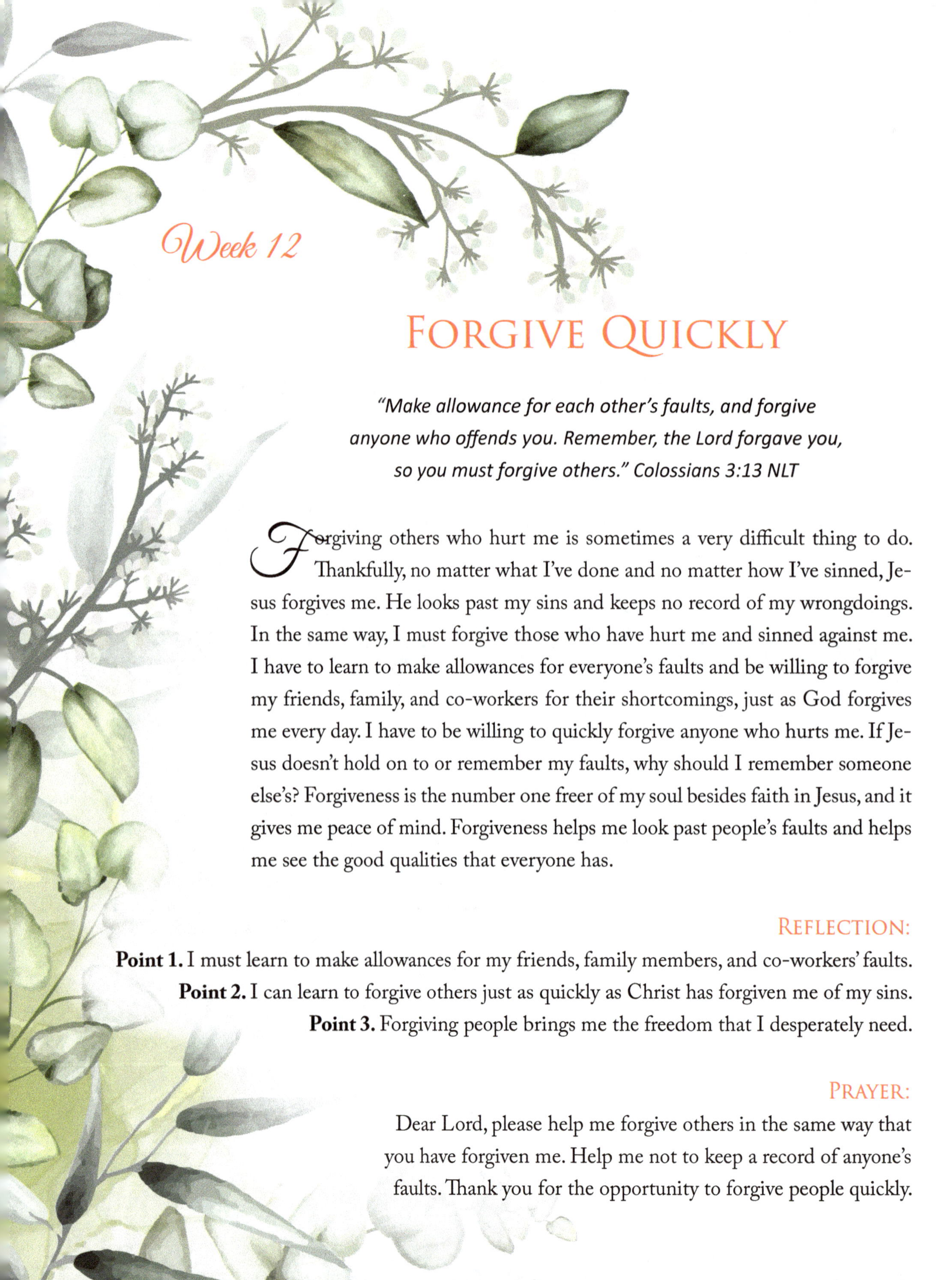

Forgive Quickly

"Make allowance for each other's faults, and forgive anyone who offends you. Remember, the Lord forgave you, so you must forgive others." Colossians 3:13 NLT

Forgiving others who hurt me is sometimes a very difficult thing to do. Thankfully, no matter what I've done and no matter how I've sinned, Jesus forgives me. He looks past my sins and keeps no record of my wrongdoings. In the same way, I must forgive those who have hurt me and sinned against me. I have to learn to make allowances for everyone's faults and be willing to forgive my friends, family, and co-workers for their shortcomings, just as God forgives me every day. I have to be willing to quickly forgive anyone who hurts me. If Jesus doesn't hold on to or remember my faults, why should I remember someone else's? Forgiveness is the number one freer of my soul besides faith in Jesus, and it gives me peace of mind. Forgiveness helps me look past people's faults and helps me see the good qualities that everyone has.

Reflection:

Point 1. I must learn to make allowances for my friends, family members, and co-workers' faults.
Point 2. I can learn to forgive others just as quickly as Christ has forgiven me of my sins.
Point 3. Forgiving people brings me the freedom that I desperately need.

Prayer:

Dear Lord, please help me forgive others in the same way that you have forgiven me. Help me not to keep a record of anyone's faults. Thank you for the opportunity to forgive people quickly.

"A friend is always loyal..." Proverbs 17:17

THINGS ON MY MIND

PRAYER REQUEST

PRAYERS ANSWERED

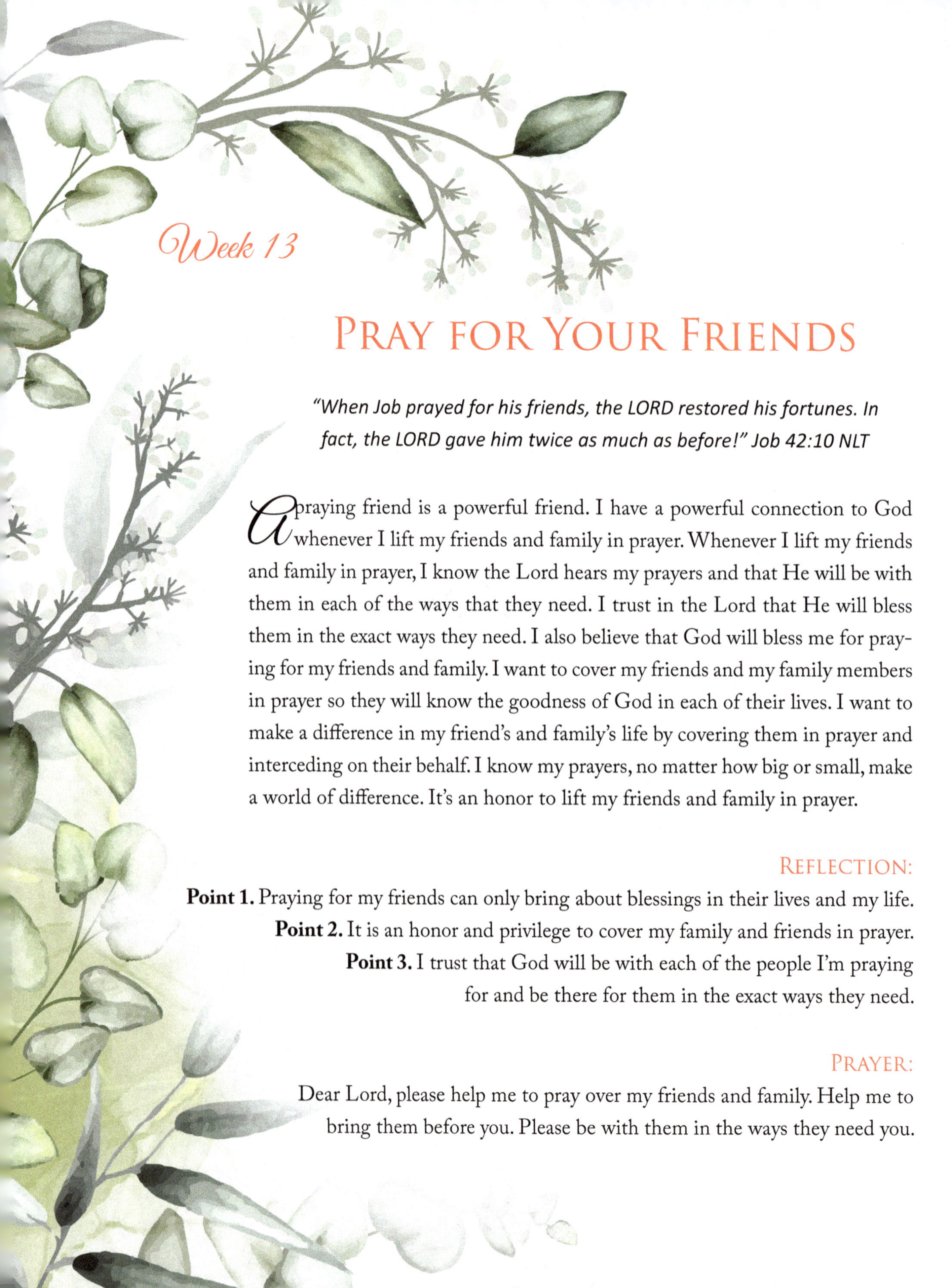

Pray for Your Friends

"When Job prayed for his friends, the LORD restored his fortunes. In fact, the LORD gave him twice as much as before!" Job 42:10 NLT

A praying friend is a powerful friend. I have a powerful connection to God whenever I lift my friends and family in prayer. Whenever I lift my friends and family in prayer, I know the Lord hears my prayers and that He will be with them in each of the ways that they need. I trust in the Lord that He will bless them in the exact ways they need. I also believe that God will bless me for praying for my friends and family. I want to cover my friends and my family members in prayer so they will know the goodness of God in each of their lives. I want to make a difference in my friend's and family's life by covering them in prayer and interceding on their behalf. I know my prayers, no matter how big or small, make a world of difference. It's an honor to lift my friends and family in prayer.

Reflection:

Point 1. Praying for my friends can only bring about blessings in their lives and my life.

Point 2. It is an honor and privilege to cover my family and friends in prayer.

Point 3. I trust that God will be with each of the people I'm praying for and be there for them in the exact ways they need.

Prayer:

Dear Lord, please help me to pray over my friends and family. Help me to bring them before you. Please be with them in the ways they need you.

"The godly give good advice to their friends..." Proverbs 12:26

THINGS ON MY MIND

PRAYER REQUEST

PRAYERS ANSWERED

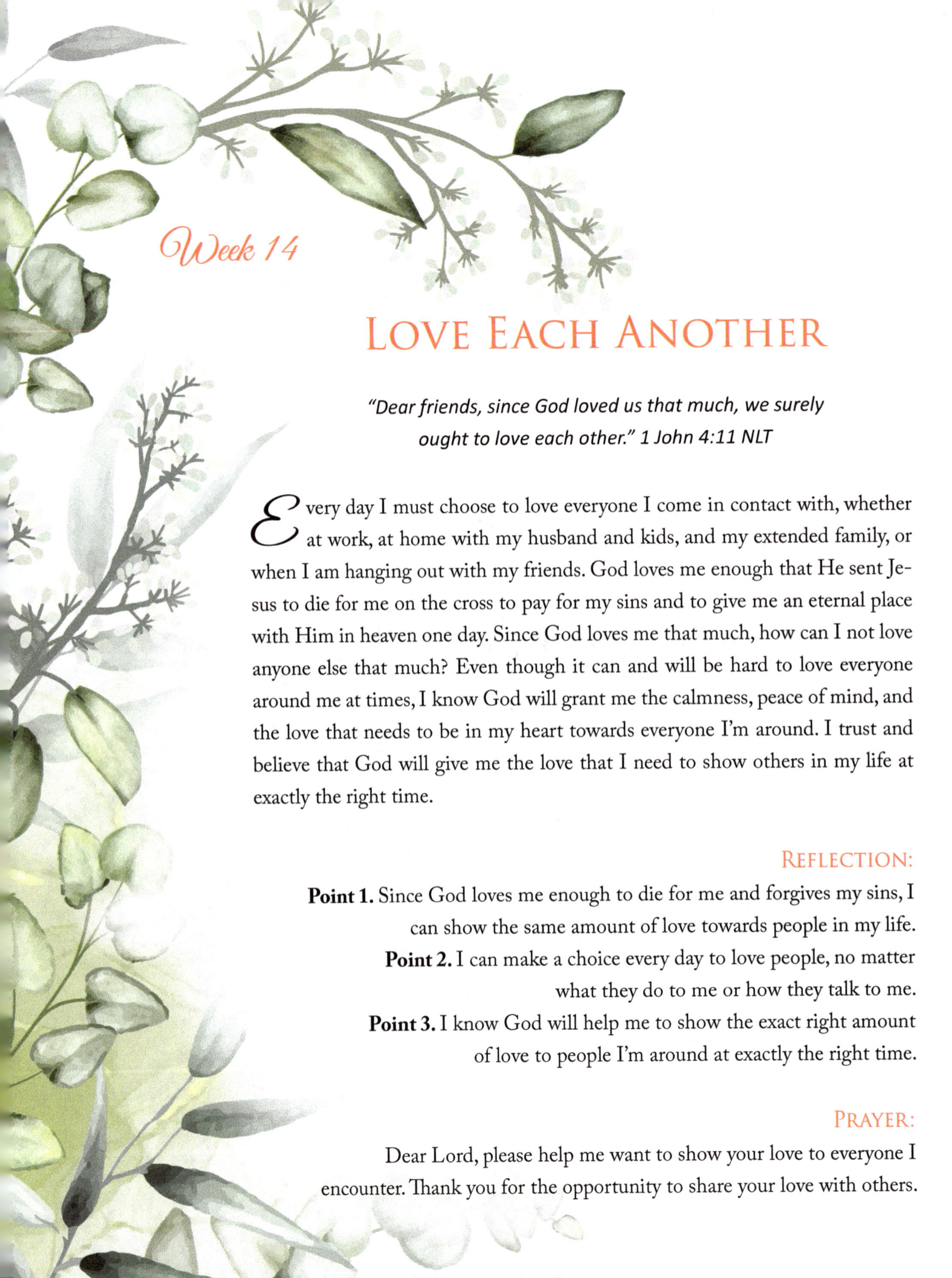

Love Each Another

*"Dear friends, since God loved us that much, we surely
ought to love each other." 1 John 4:11 NLT*

Every day I must choose to love everyone I come in contact with, whether at work, at home with my husband and kids, and my extended family, or when I am hanging out with my friends. God loves me enough that He sent Jesus to die for me on the cross to pay for my sins and to give me an eternal place with Him in heaven one day. Since God loves me that much, how can I not love anyone else that much? Even though it can and will be hard to love everyone around me at times, I know God will grant me the calmness, peace of mind, and the love that needs to be in my heart towards everyone I'm around. I trust and believe that God will give me the love that I need to show others in my life at exactly the right time.

Reflection:

Point 1. Since God loves me enough to die for me and forgives my sins, I can show the same amount of love towards people in my life.

Point 2. I can make a choice every day to love people, no matter what they do to me or how they talk to me.

Point 3. I know God will help me to show the exact right amount of love to people I'm around at exactly the right time.

Prayer:

Dear Lord, please help me want to show your love to everyone I encounter. Thank you for the opportunity to share your love with others.

"Love never fails."
1 Corinthians 4:8

THINGS ON MY MIND

PRAYER REQUEST

PRAYERS ANSWERED

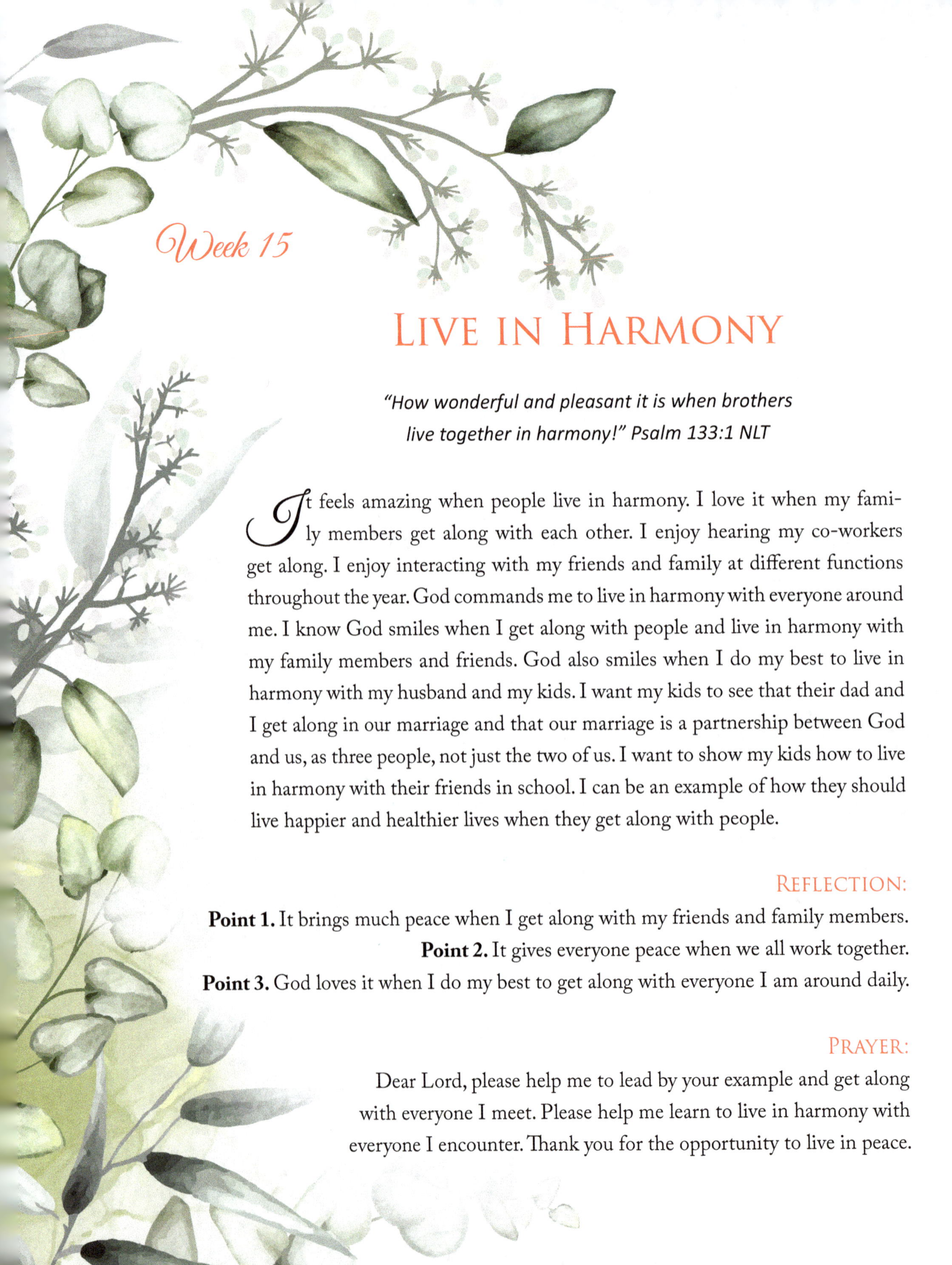

Live in Harmony

*"How wonderful and pleasant it is when brothers
live together in harmony!" Psalm 133:1 NLT*

It feels amazing when people live in harmony. I love it when my family members get along with each other. I enjoy hearing my co-workers get along. I enjoy interacting with my friends and family at different functions throughout the year. God commands me to live in harmony with everyone around me. I know God smiles when I get along with people and live in harmony with my family members and friends. God also smiles when I do my best to live in harmony with my husband and my kids. I want my kids to see that their dad and I get along in our marriage and that our marriage is a partnership between God and us, as three people, not just the two of us. I want to show my kids how to live in harmony with their friends in school. I can be an example of how they should live happier and healthier lives when they get along with people.

Reflection:

Point 1. It brings much peace when I get along with my friends and family members.

Point 2. It gives everyone peace when we all work together.

Point 3. God loves it when I do my best to get along with everyone I am around daily.

Prayer:

Dear Lord, please help me to lead by your example and get along with everyone I meet. Please help me learn to live in harmony with everyone I encounter. Thank you for the opportunity to live in peace.

"…Love your neighbor as yourself" Romans 13:9

THINGS ON MY MIND

PRAYER REQUEST

PRAYERS ANSWERED

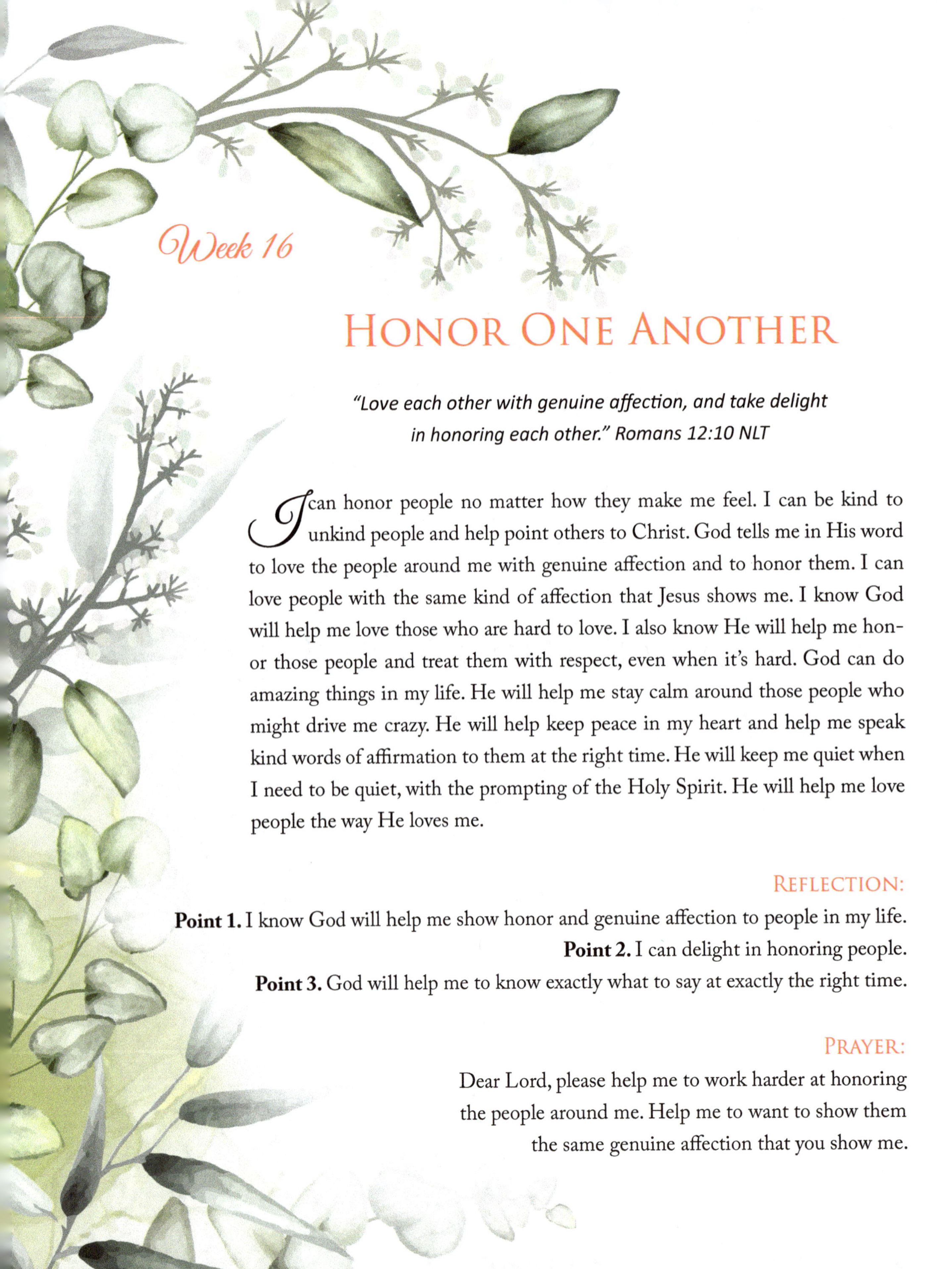

HONOR ONE ANOTHER

"Love each other with genuine affection, and take delight in honoring each other." Romans 12:10 NLT

I can honor people no matter how they make me feel. I can be kind to unkind people and help point others to Christ. God tells me in His word to love the people around me with genuine affection and to honor them. I can love people with the same kind of affection that Jesus shows me. I know God will help me love those who are hard to love. I also know He will help me honor those people and treat them with respect, even when it's hard. God can do amazing things in my life. He will help me stay calm around those people who might drive me crazy. He will help keep peace in my heart and help me speak kind words of affirmation to them at the right time. He will keep me quiet when I need to be quiet, with the prompting of the Holy Spirit. He will help me love people the way He loves me.

REFLECTION:

Point 1. I know God will help me show honor and genuine affection to people in my life.

Point 2. I can delight in honoring people.

Point 3. God will help me to know exactly what to say at exactly the right time.

PRAYER:

Dear Lord, please help me to work harder at honoring the people around me. Help me to want to show them the same genuine affection that you show me.

"We love because he first loved us." 1 John 4:19

THINGS ON MY MIND

PRAYER REQUEST	PRAYERS ANSWERED

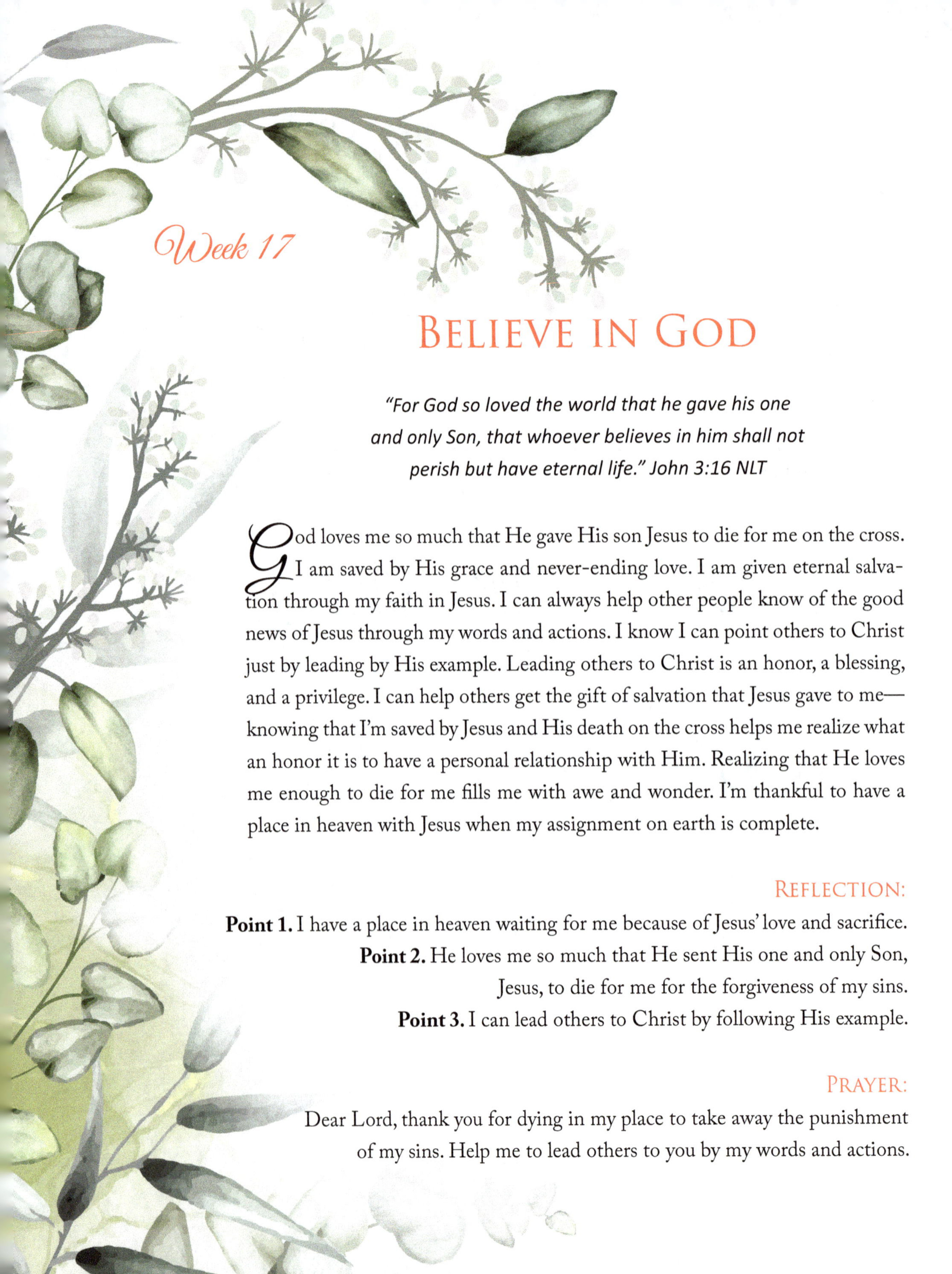

Believe in God

"For God so loved the world that he gave his one and only Son, that whoever believes in him shall not perish but have eternal life." John 3:16 NLT

God loves me so much that He gave His son Jesus to die for me on the cross. I am saved by His grace and never-ending love. I am given eternal salvation through my faith in Jesus. I can always help other people know of the good news of Jesus through my words and actions. I know I can point others to Christ just by leading by His example. Leading others to Christ is an honor, a blessing, and a privilege. I can help others get the gift of salvation that Jesus gave to me—knowing that I'm saved by Jesus and His death on the cross helps me realize what an honor it is to have a personal relationship with Him. Realizing that He loves me enough to die for me fills me with awe and wonder. I'm thankful to have a place in heaven with Jesus when my assignment on earth is complete.

REFLECTION:

Point 1. I have a place in heaven waiting for me because of Jesus' love and sacrifice.

Point 2. He loves me so much that He sent His one and only Son, Jesus, to die for me for the forgiveness of my sins.

Point 3. I can lead others to Christ by following His example.

PRAYER:

Dear Lord, thank you for dying in my place to take away the punishment of my sins. Help me to lead others to you by my words and actions.

"Let all that you do be done in love."
1 Corinthians 16:14

THINGS ON MY MIND

PRAYER REQUEST

PRAYERS ANSWERED

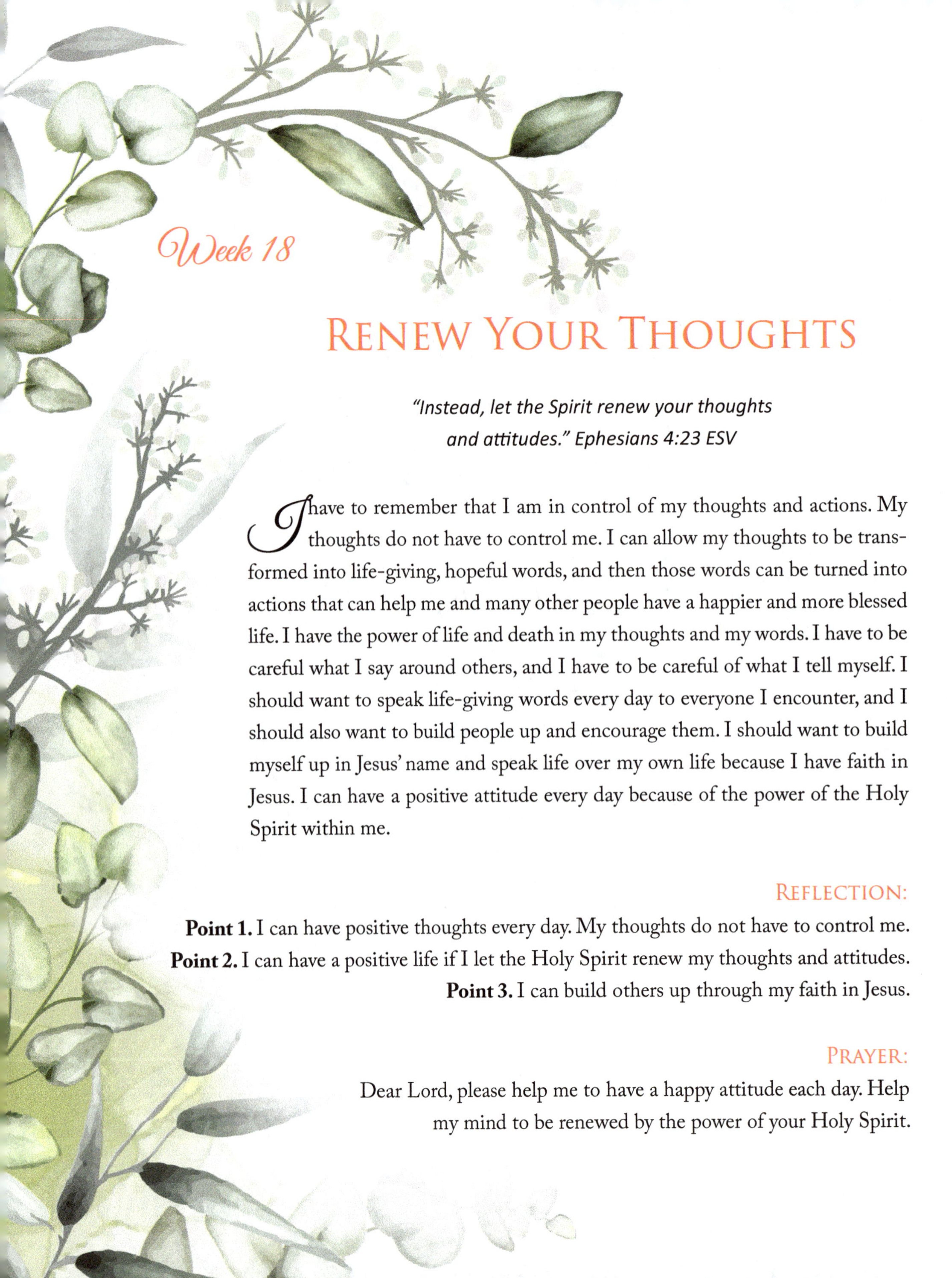

Renew Your Thoughts

"Instead, let the Spirit renew your thoughts and attitudes." Ephesians 4:23 ESV

I have to remember that I am in control of my thoughts and actions. My thoughts do not have to control me. I can allow my thoughts to be transformed into life-giving, hopeful words, and then those words can be turned into actions that can help me and many other people have a happier and more blessed life. I have the power of life and death in my thoughts and my words. I have to be careful what I say around others, and I have to be careful of what I tell myself. I should want to speak life-giving words every day to everyone I encounter, and I should also want to build people up and encourage them. I should want to build myself up in Jesus' name and speak life over my own life because I have faith in Jesus. I can have a positive attitude every day because of the power of the Holy Spirit within me.

Reflection:

Point 1. I can have positive thoughts every day. My thoughts do not have to control me.
Point 2. I can have a positive life if I let the Holy Spirit renew my thoughts and attitudes.
Point 3. I can build others up through my faith in Jesus.

Prayer:

Dear Lord, please help me to have a happy attitude each day. Help my mind to be renewed by the power of your Holy Spirit.

"Pray without ceasing."
1 Thessalonians 5:17

THINGS ON MY MIND

PRAYER REQUEST

PRAYERS ANSWERED

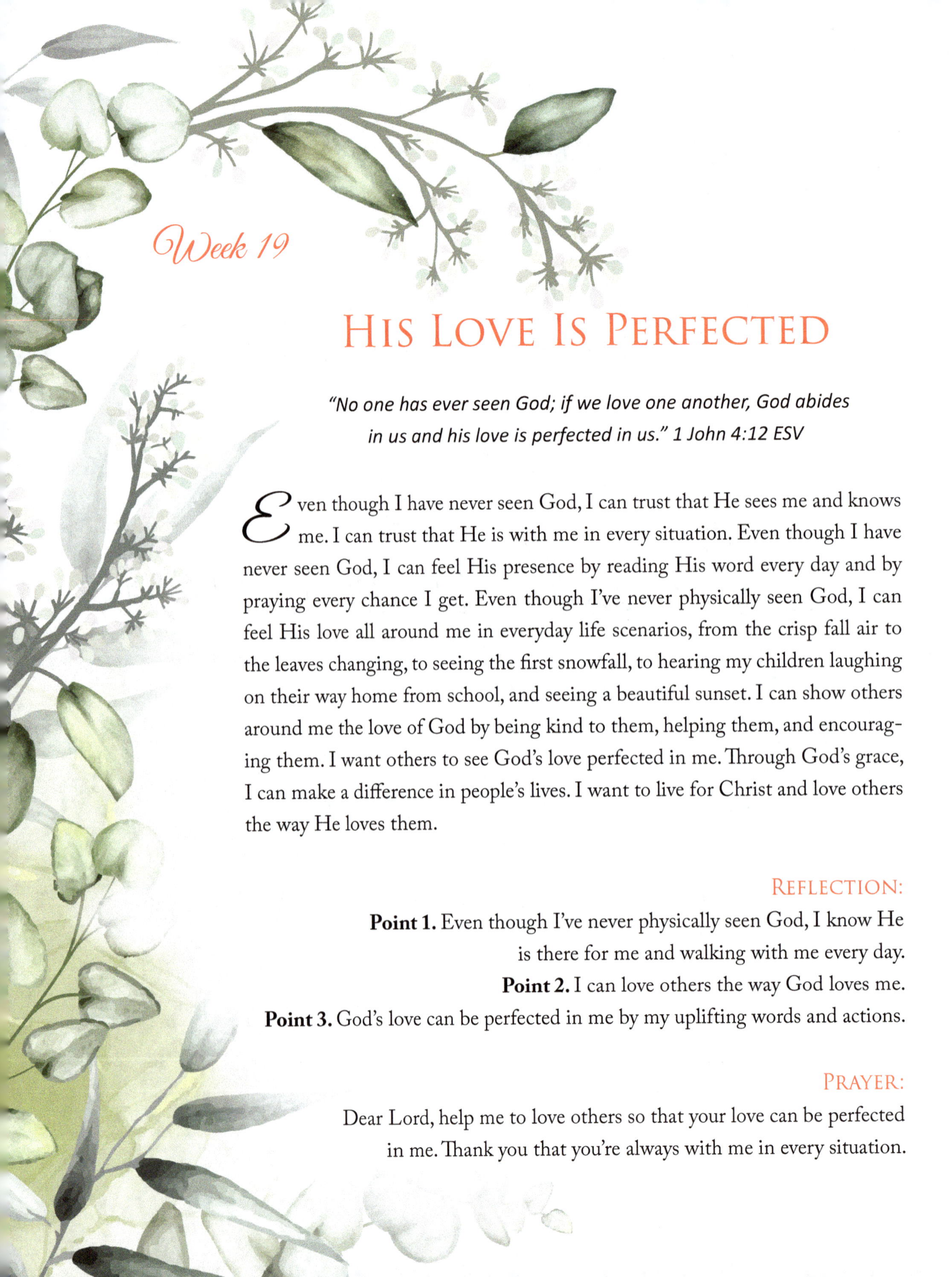

His Love Is Perfected

"No one has ever seen God; if we love one another, God abides in us and his love is perfected in us." 1 John 4:12 ESV

Even though I have never seen God, I can trust that He sees me and knows me. I can trust that He is with me in every situation. Even though I have never seen God, I can feel His presence by reading His word every day and by praying every chance I get. Even though I've never physically seen God, I can feel His love all around me in everyday life scenarios, from the crisp fall air to the leaves changing, to seeing the first snowfall, to hearing my children laughing on their way home from school, and seeing a beautiful sunset. I can show others around me the love of God by being kind to them, helping them, and encouraging them. I want others to see God's love perfected in me. Through God's grace, I can make a difference in people's lives. I want to live for Christ and love others the way He loves them.

REFLECTION:

Point 1. Even though I've never physically seen God, I know He is there for me and walking with me every day.
Point 2. I can love others the way God loves me.
Point 3. God's love can be perfected in me by my uplifting words and actions.

PRAYER:

Dear Lord, help me to love others so that your love can be perfected in me. Thank you that you're always with me in every situation.

"Seek the Lord and his strength; seek his presence continually!"
1 Chronicles 16:11

THINGS ON MY MIND

PRAYER REQUEST

PRAYERS ANSWERED

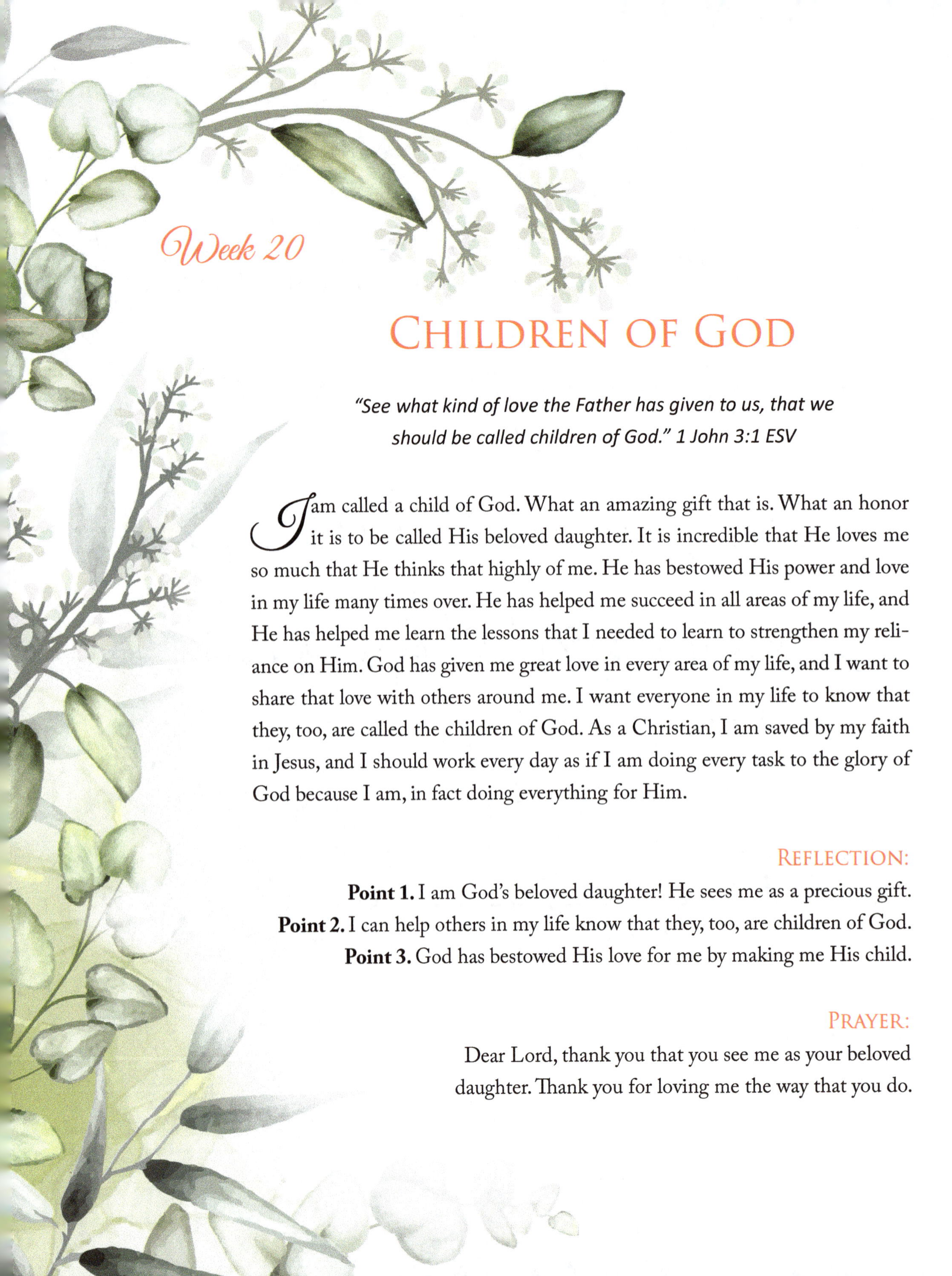

CHILDREN OF GOD

"See what kind of love the Father has given to us, that we should be called children of God." 1 John 3:1 ESV

I am called a child of God. What an amazing gift that is. What an honor it is to be called His beloved daughter. It is incredible that He loves me so much that He thinks that highly of me. He has bestowed His power and love in my life many times over. He has helped me succeed in all areas of my life, and He has helped me learn the lessons that I needed to learn to strengthen my reliance on Him. God has given me great love in every area of my life, and I want to share that love with others around me. I want everyone in my life to know that they, too, are called the children of God. As a Christian, I am saved by my faith in Jesus, and I should work every day as if I am doing every task to the glory of God because I am, in fact doing everything for Him.

REFLECTION:

Point 1. I am God's beloved daughter! He sees me as a precious gift.
Point 2. I can help others in my life know that they, too, are children of God.
Point 3. God has bestowed His love for me by making me His child.

PRAYER:

Dear Lord, thank you that you see me as your beloved daughter. Thank you for loving me the way that you do.

"So, glorify God in your body."
1 Corinthians 6:20

THINGS ON MY MIND

PRAYER REQUEST

PRAYERS ANSWERED

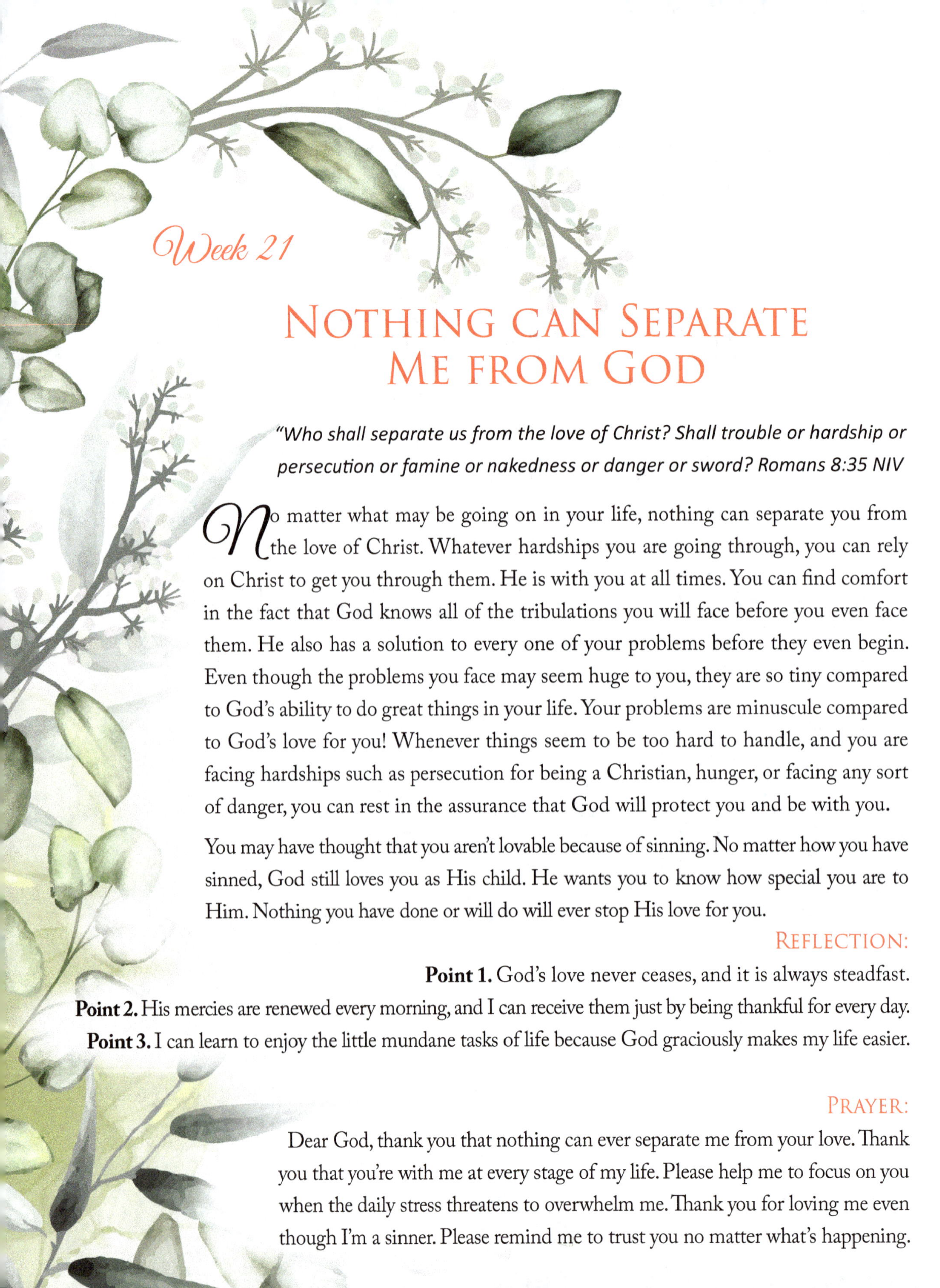

Nothing can Separate Me from God

"Who shall separate us from the love of Christ? Shall trouble or hardship or persecution or famine or nakedness or danger or sword? Romans 8:35 NIV

No matter what may be going on in your life, nothing can separate you from the love of Christ. Whatever hardships you are going through, you can rely on Christ to get you through them. He is with you at all times. You can find comfort in the fact that God knows all of the tribulations you will face before you even face them. He also has a solution to every one of your problems before they even begin. Even though the problems you face may seem huge to you, they are so tiny compared to God's ability to do great things in your life. Your problems are minuscule compared to God's love for you! Whenever things seem to be too hard to handle, and you are facing hardships such as persecution for being a Christian, hunger, or facing any sort of danger, you can rest in the assurance that God will protect you and be with you.

You may have thought that you aren't lovable because of sinning. No matter how you have sinned, God still loves you as His child. He wants you to know how special you are to Him. Nothing you have done or will do will ever stop His love for you.

Reflection:

Point 1. God's love never ceases, and it is always steadfast.

Point 2. His mercies are renewed every morning, and I can receive them just by being thankful for every day.

Point 3. I can learn to enjoy the little mundane tasks of life because God graciously makes my life easier.

Prayer:

Dear God, thank you that nothing can ever separate me from your love. Thank you that you're with me at every stage of my life. Please help me to focus on you when the daily stress threatens to overwhelm me. Thank you for loving me even though I'm a sinner. Please remind me to trust you no matter what's happening.

"...his steadfast love endures forever." Psalm 136:26

THINGS ON MY MIND

PRAYER REQUEST

PRAYERS ANSWERED

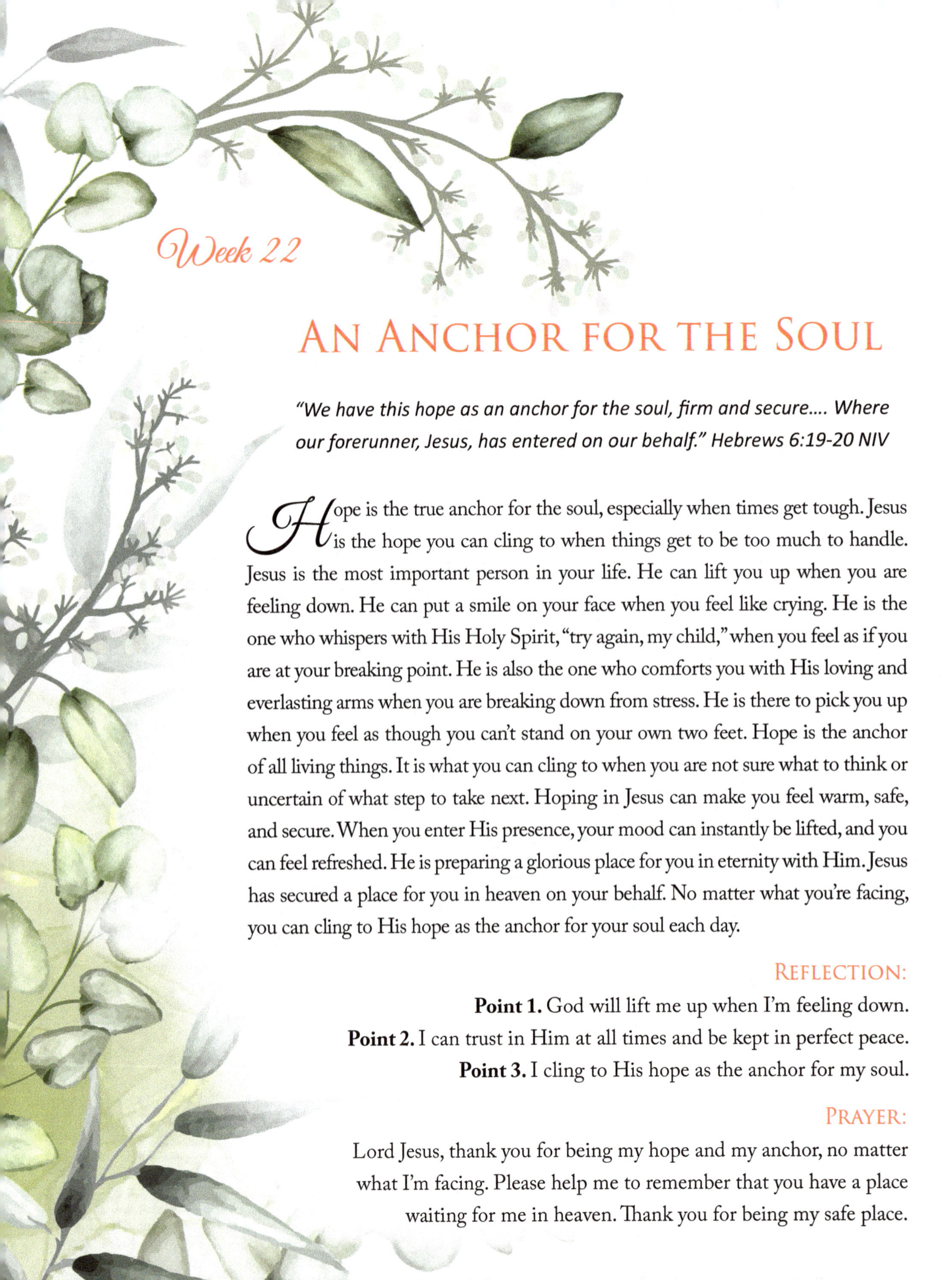

An Anchor for the Soul

"We have this hope as an anchor for the soul, firm and secure.… Where our forerunner, Jesus, has entered on our behalf." Hebrews 6:19-20 NIV

Hope is the true anchor for the soul, especially when times get tough. Jesus is the hope you can cling to when things get to be too much to handle. Jesus is the most important person in your life. He can lift you up when you are feeling down. He can put a smile on your face when you feel like crying. He is the one who whispers with His Holy Spirit, "try again, my child," when you feel as if you are at your breaking point. He is also the one who comforts you with His loving and everlasting arms when you are breaking down from stress. He is there to pick you up when you feel as though you can't stand on your own two feet. Hope is the anchor of all living things. It is what you can cling to when you are not sure what to think or uncertain of what step to take next. Hoping in Jesus can make you feel warm, safe, and secure. When you enter His presence, your mood can instantly be lifted, and you can feel refreshed. He is preparing a glorious place for you in eternity with Him. Jesus has secured a place for you in heaven on your behalf. No matter what you're facing, you can cling to His hope as the anchor for your soul each day.

Reflection:

Point 1. God will lift me up when I'm feeling down.

Point 2. I can trust in Him at all times and be kept in perfect peace.

Point 3. I cling to His hope as the anchor for my soul.

Prayer:

Lord Jesus, thank you for being my hope and my anchor, no matter what I'm facing. Please help me to remember that you have a place waiting for me in heaven. Thank you for being my safe place.

"Mercy, peace and love be yours in abundance."
Jude 1:2

THINGS ON MY MIND

PRAYER REQUEST

PRAYERS ANSWERED

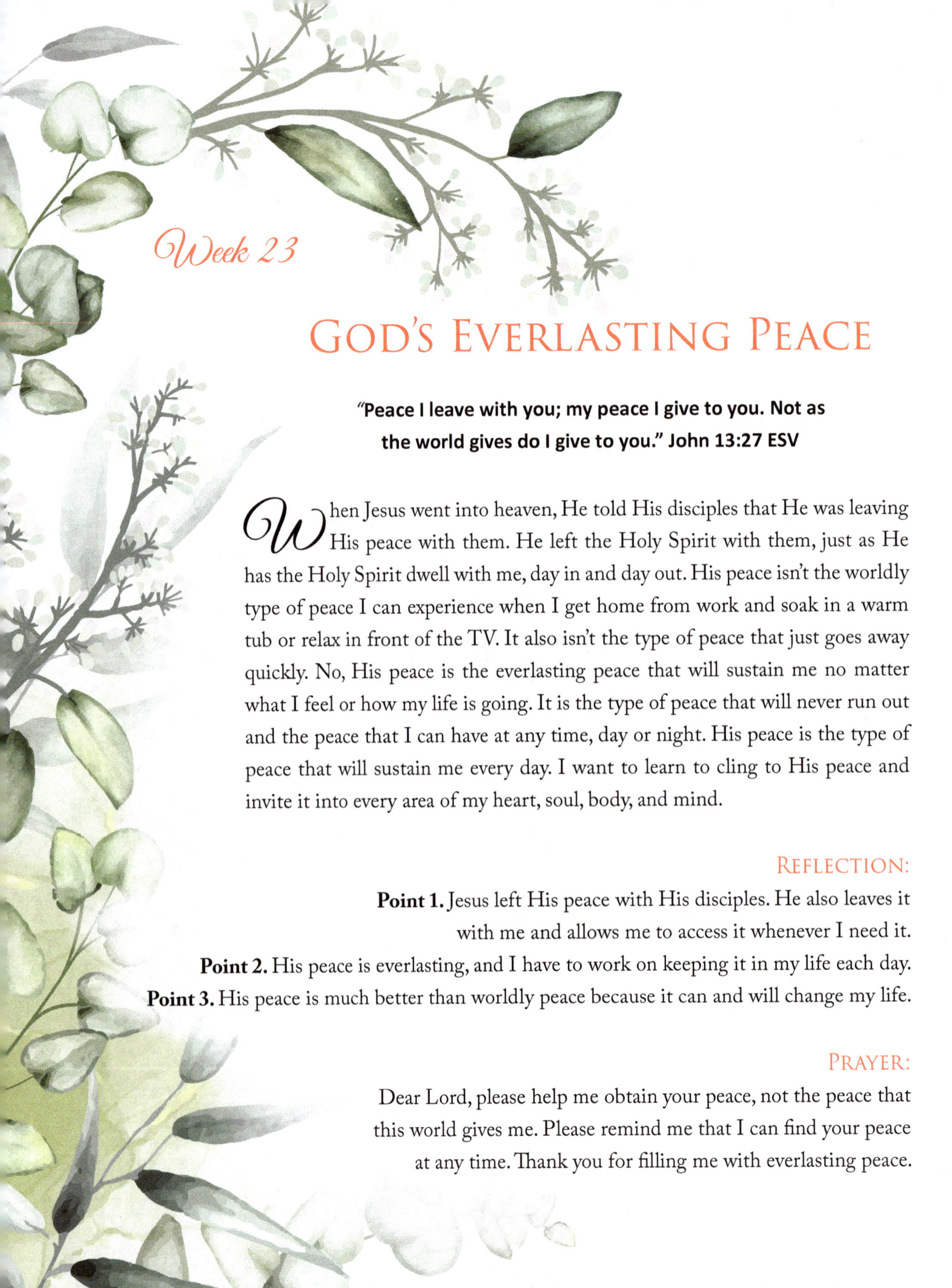

God's Everlasting Peace

"Peace I leave with you; my peace I give to you. Not as the world gives do I give to you." John 13:27 ESV

When Jesus went into heaven, He told His disciples that He was leaving His peace with them. He left the Holy Spirit with them, just as He has the Holy Spirit dwell with me, day in and day out. His peace isn't the worldly type of peace I can experience when I get home from work and soak in a warm tub or relax in front of the TV. It also isn't the type of peace that just goes away quickly. No, His peace is the everlasting peace that will sustain me no matter what I feel or how my life is going. It is the type of peace that will never run out and the peace that I can have at any time, day or night. His peace is the type of peace that will sustain me every day. I want to learn to cling to His peace and invite it into every area of my heart, soul, body, and mind.

Reflection:

Point 1. Jesus left His peace with His disciples. He also leaves it with me and allows me to access it whenever I need it.

Point 2. His peace is everlasting, and I have to work on keeping it in my life each day.

Point 3. His peace is much better than worldly peace because it can and will change my life.

Prayer:

Dear Lord, please help me obtain your peace, not the peace that this world gives me. Please remind me that I can find your peace at any time. Thank you for filling me with everlasting peace.

"In his days may the righteous flourish..." Psalm 72:7

Things on My Mind

Prayer Request

Prayers Answered

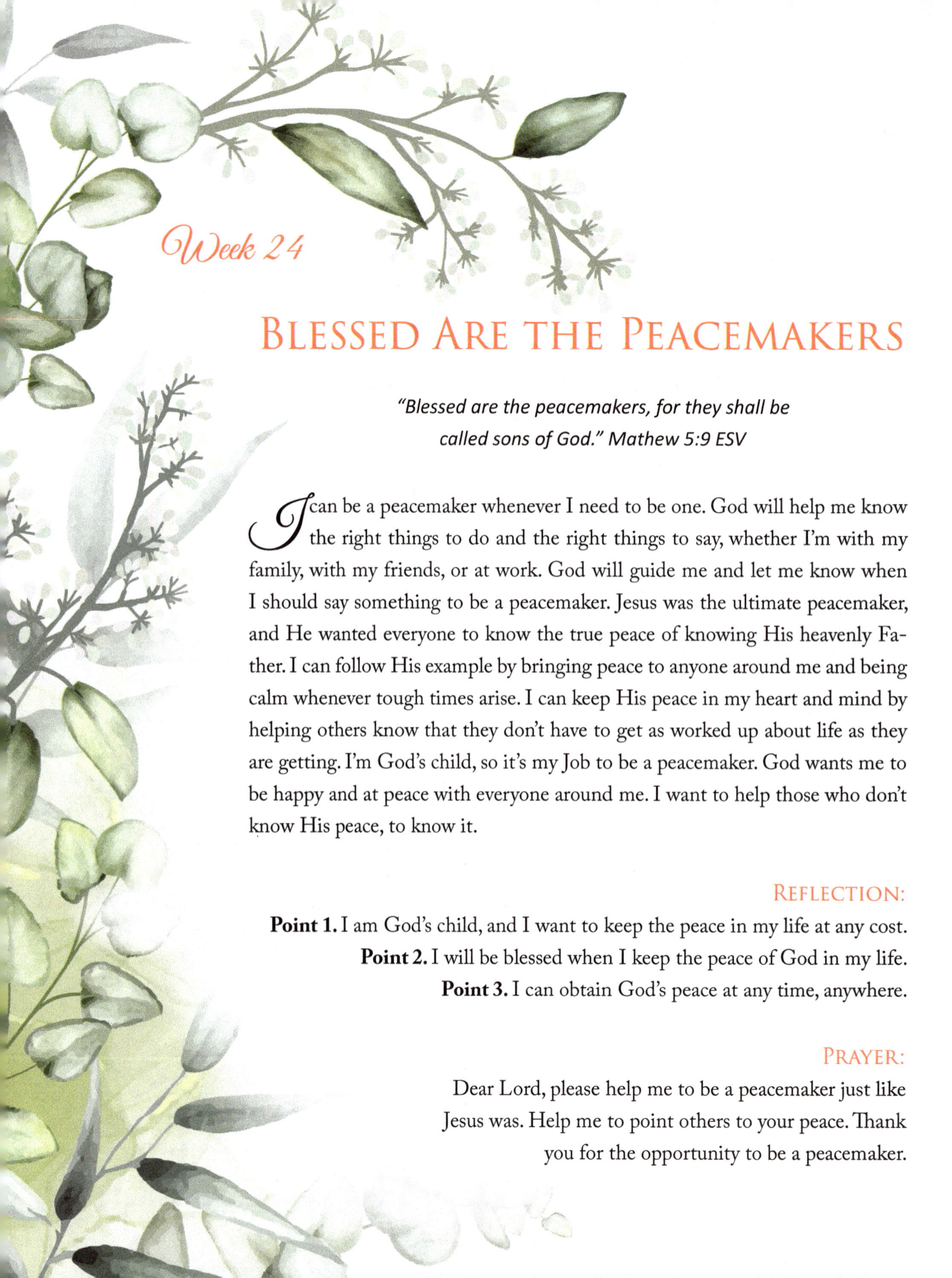

Blessed Are the Peacemakers

*"Blessed are the peacemakers, for they shall be
called sons of God." Mathew 5:9 ESV*

I can be a peacemaker whenever I need to be one. God will help me know the right things to do and the right things to say, whether I'm with my family, with my friends, or at work. God will guide me and let me know when I should say something to be a peacemaker. Jesus was the ultimate peacemaker, and He wanted everyone to know the true peace of knowing His heavenly Father. I can follow His example by bringing peace to anyone around me and being calm whenever tough times arise. I can keep His peace in my heart and mind by helping others know that they don't have to get as worked up about life as they are getting. I'm God's child, so it's my Job to be a peacemaker. God wants me to be happy and at peace with everyone around me. I want to help those who don't know His peace, to know it.

Reflection:

Point 1. I am God's child, and I want to keep the peace in my life at any cost.
Point 2. I will be blessed when I keep the peace of God in my life.
Point 3. I can obtain God's peace at any time, anywhere.

Prayer:

Dear Lord, please help me to be a peacemaker just like
Jesus was. Help me to point others to your peace. Thank
you for the opportunity to be a peacemaker.

"These things have I spoken unto you, that in me ye may have peace..." John 16:33

THINGS ON MY MIND

PRAYER REQUEST

PRAYERS ANSWERED

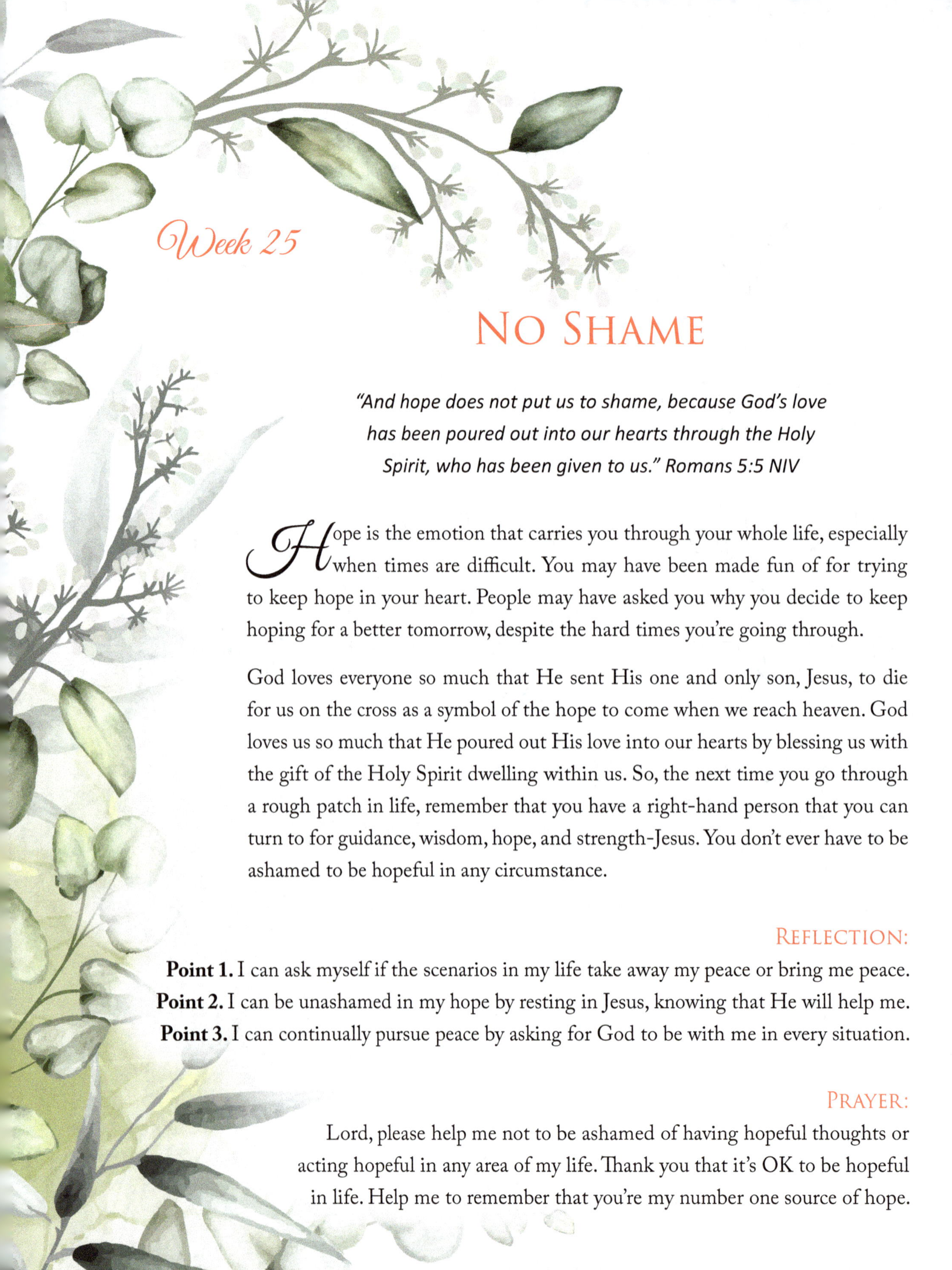

No Shame

"And hope does not put us to shame, because God's love has been poured out into our hearts through the Holy Spirit, who has been given to us." Romans 5:5 NIV

Hope is the emotion that carries you through your whole life, especially when times are difficult. You may have been made fun of for trying to keep hope in your heart. People may have asked you why you decide to keep hoping for a better tomorrow, despite the hard times you're going through.

God loves everyone so much that He sent His one and only son, Jesus, to die for us on the cross as a symbol of the hope to come when we reach heaven. God loves us so much that He poured out His love into our hearts by blessing us with the gift of the Holy Spirit dwelling within us. So, the next time you go through a rough patch in life, remember that you have a right-hand person that you can turn to for guidance, wisdom, hope, and strength-Jesus. You don't ever have to be ashamed to be hopeful in any circumstance.

Reflection:

Point 1. I can ask myself if the scenarios in my life take away my peace or bring me peace.
Point 2. I can be unashamed in my hope by resting in Jesus, knowing that He will help me.
Point 3. I can continually pursue peace by asking for God to be with me in every situation.

Prayer:

Lord, please help me not to be ashamed of having hopeful thoughts or acting hopeful in any area of my life. Thank you that it's OK to be hopeful in life. Help me to remember that you're my number one source of hope.

"And let the peace of Christ rule in your hearts..." Colossians 3:15

Things on My Mind

Prayer Request

Prayers Answered

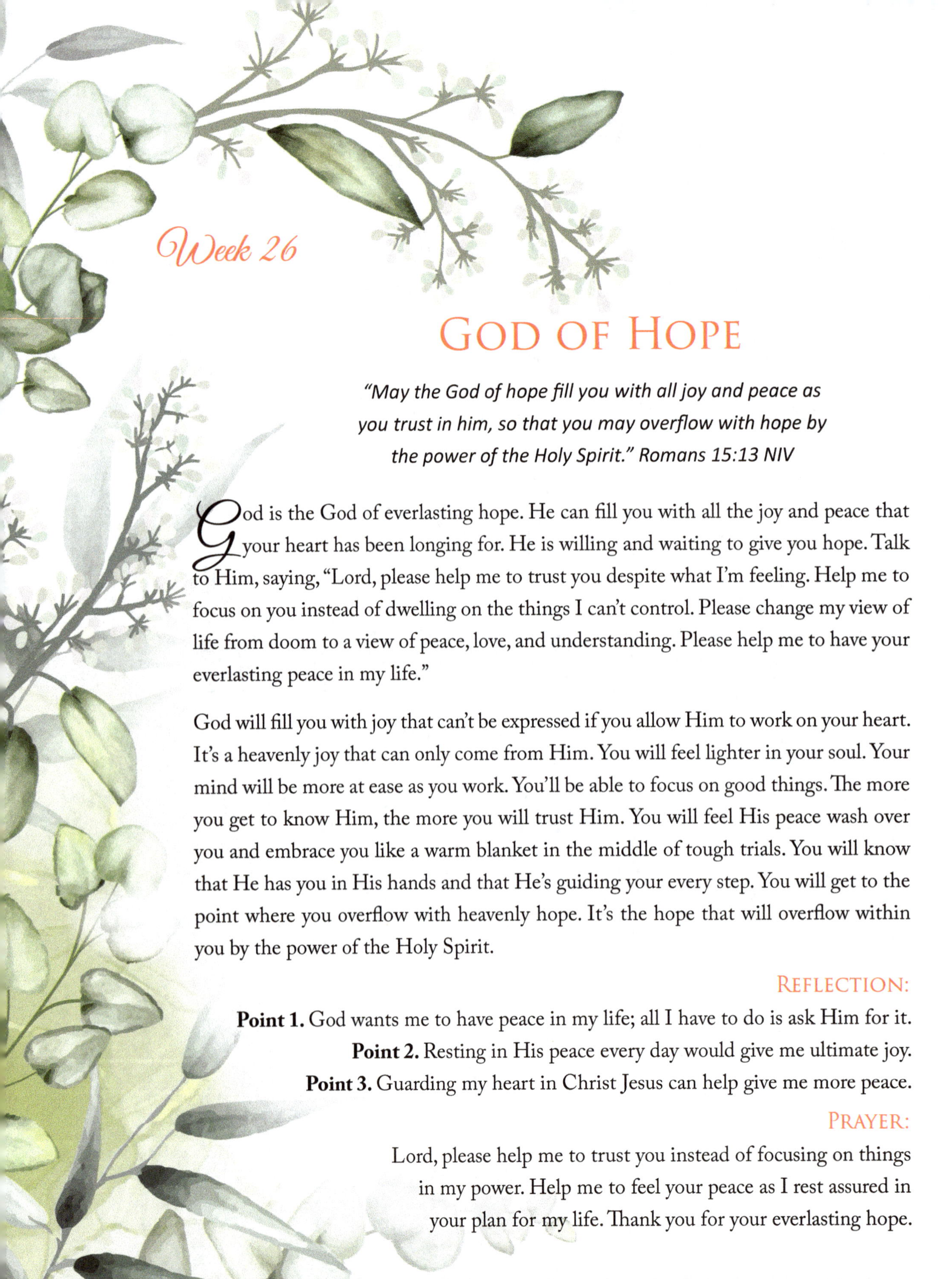

GOD OF HOPE

"May the God of hope fill you with all joy and peace as you trust in him, so that you may overflow with hope by the power of the Holy Spirit." Romans 15:13 NIV

God is the God of everlasting hope. He can fill you with all the joy and peace that your heart has been longing for. He is willing and waiting to give you hope. Talk to Him, saying, "Lord, please help me to trust you despite what I'm feeling. Help me to focus on you instead of dwelling on the things I can't control. Please change my view of life from doom to a view of peace, love, and understanding. Please help me to have your everlasting peace in my life."

God will fill you with joy that can't be expressed if you allow Him to work on your heart. It's a heavenly joy that can only come from Him. You will feel lighter in your soul. Your mind will be more at ease as you work. You'll be able to focus on good things. The more you get to know Him, the more you will trust Him. You will feel His peace wash over you and embrace you like a warm blanket in the middle of tough trials. You will know that He has you in His hands and that He's guiding your every step. You will get to the point where you overflow with heavenly hope. It's the hope that will overflow within you by the power of the Holy Spirit.

REFLECTION:

Point 1. God wants me to have peace in my life; all I have to do is ask Him for it.

Point 2. Resting in His peace every day would give me ultimate joy.

Point 3. Guarding my heart in Christ Jesus can help give me more peace.

PRAYER:

Lord, please help me to trust you instead of focusing on things in my power. Help me to feel your peace as I rest assured in your plan for my life. Thank you for your everlasting hope.

"...And I will give peace in the land..."
Leviticus 26:6

THINGS ON MY MIND

PRAYER REQUEST

PRAYERS ANSWERED

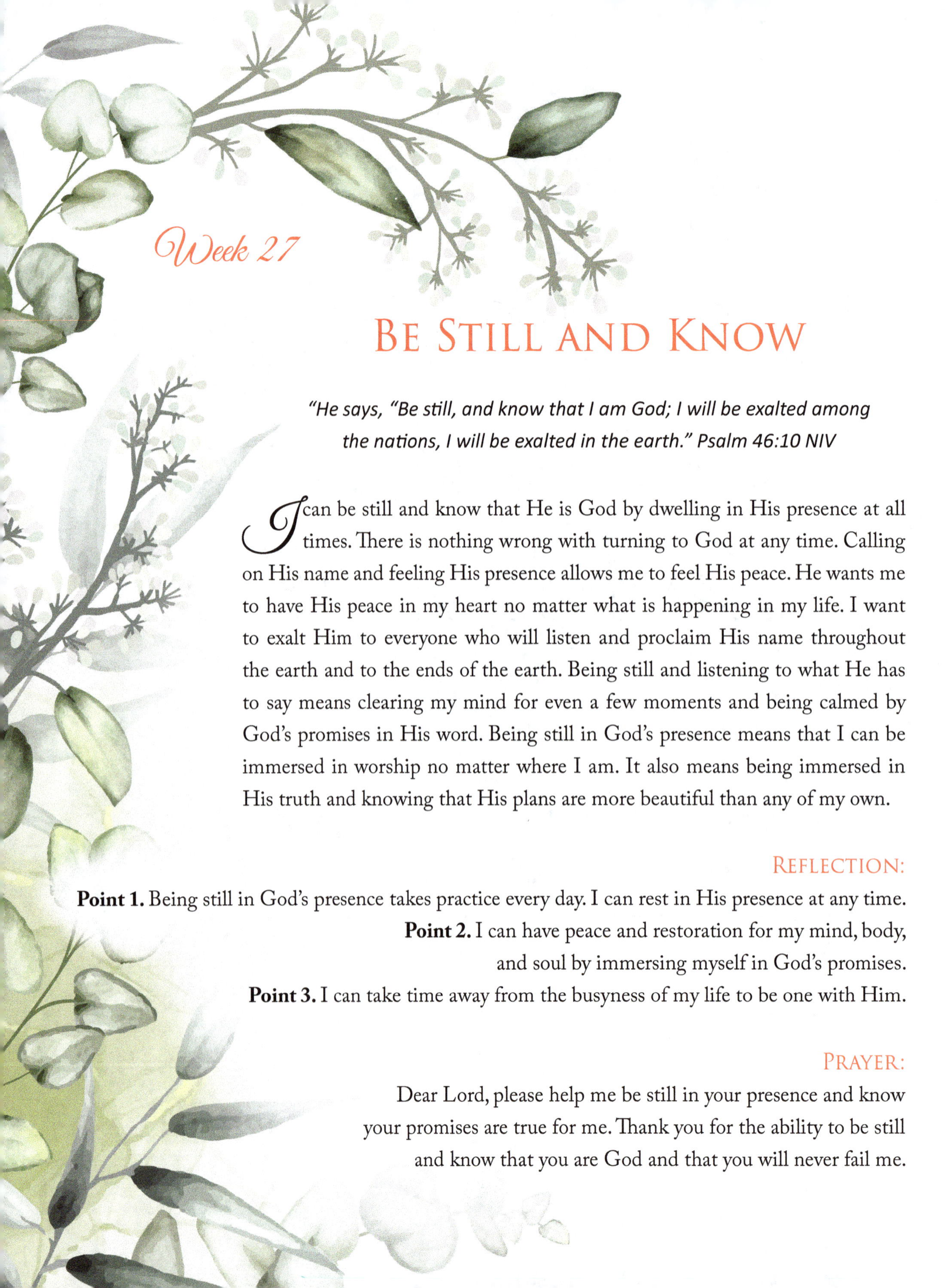

Be Still and Know

"He says, "Be still, and know that I am God; I will be exalted among the nations, I will be exalted in the earth." Psalm 46:10 NIV

I can be still and know that He is God by dwelling in His presence at all times. There is nothing wrong with turning to God at any time. Calling on His name and feeling His presence allows me to feel His peace. He wants me to have His peace in my heart no matter what is happening in my life. I want to exalt Him to everyone who will listen and proclaim His name throughout the earth and to the ends of the earth. Being still and listening to what He has to say means clearing my mind for even a few moments and being calmed by God's promises in His word. Being still in God's presence means that I can be immersed in worship no matter where I am. It also means being immersed in His truth and knowing that His plans are more beautiful than any of my own.

Reflection:

Point 1. Being still in God's presence takes practice every day. I can rest in His presence at any time.

Point 2. I can have peace and restoration for my mind, body, and soul by immersing myself in God's promises.

Point 3. I can take time away from the busyness of my life to be one with Him.

Prayer:

Dear Lord, please help me be still in your presence and know your promises are true for me. Thank you for the ability to be still and know that you are God and that you will never fail me.

"Praise the LORD, my soul..." Psalm 103:1

THINGS ON MY MIND

PRAYER REQUEST

PRAYERS ANSWERED

Sleep in Peace

"In peace will I both lay me down and sleep; For thou, Jehovah, alone makest me dwell in safety." Psalm 4:8 ASV

I don't have to be afraid of anything because God wants me to rest every night, no matter what is going on. I know I am kept safe in every situation because God is with me. God wants me to rest assured in His promises that He makes to me in this scripture. He allows me to lie down in safety every night, no matter where I sleep. He gives me the option to choose His peace and rest every night after a long day of work. He wants me to know that I can get good restful sleep every night, even when I sometimes think I won't be able to. All I have to do is call on His name and ask for His peace to fill my heart. He will allow me to get sleep so I can be more productive with my time every day. I want to lie down and sleep in His peace.

Reflection:

Point 1. God lets me know that I can lie down and sleep in peace every night. He is protecting me.

Point 2. It is my choice whether or not I choose to lie down and sleep in peace every night.

Point 3. God loves me enough that He assures me that I can always rest soundly every night.

Prayer:

Dear Lord, please help me to sleep soundly every night. Thank you for protecting me in every way and for allowing me to sleep in peace.

"...Thy lovingkindness, O Jehovah, endureth forever;" Psalm 138:8

THINGS ON MY MIND

PRAYER REQUEST

PRAYERS ANSWERED

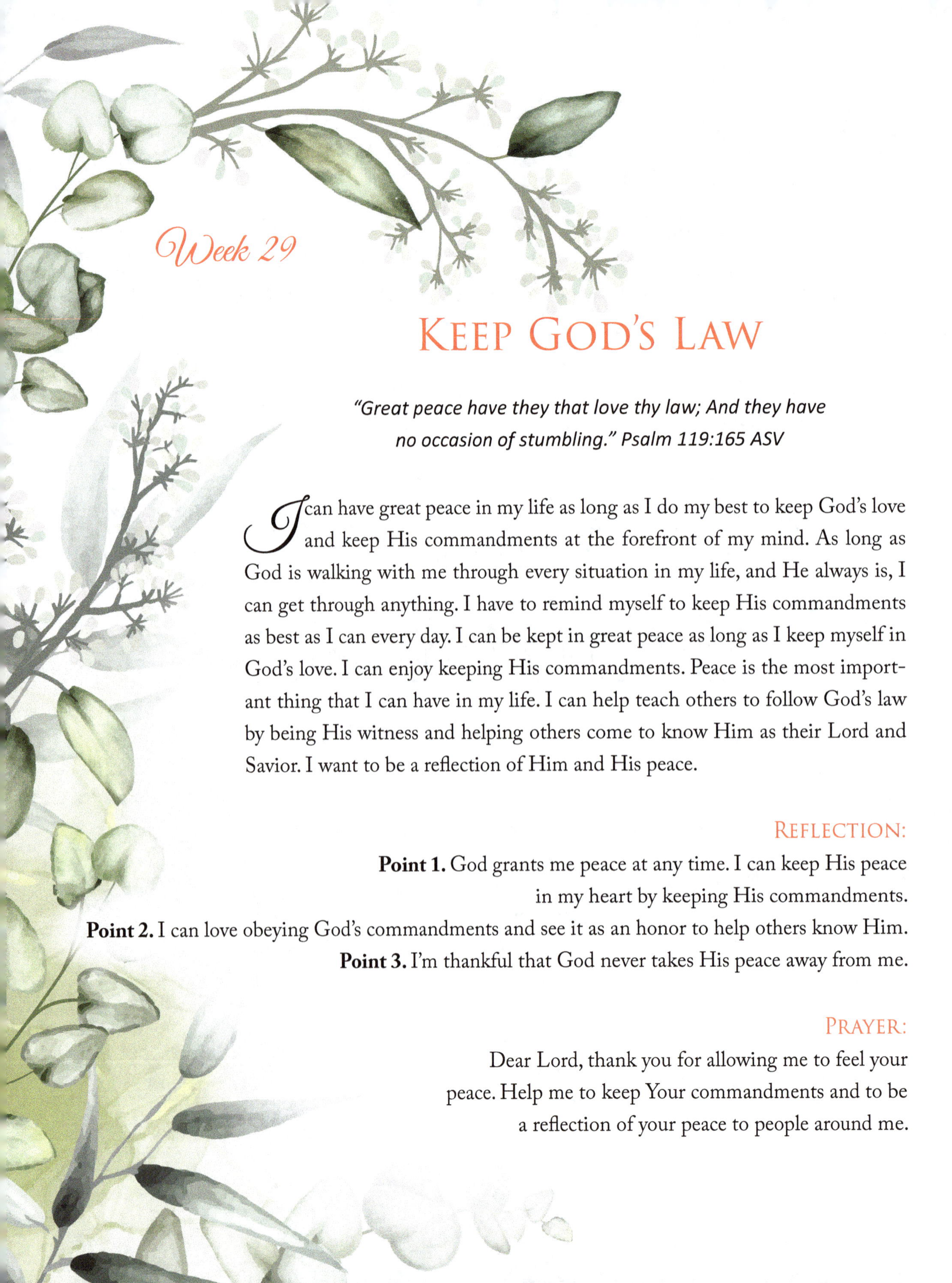

Keep God's Law

*"Great peace have they that love thy law; And they have
no occasion of stumbling." Psalm 119:165 ASV*

I can have great peace in my life as long as I do my best to keep God's love and keep His commandments at the forefront of my mind. As long as God is walking with me through every situation in my life, and He always is, I can get through anything. I have to remind myself to keep His commandments as best as I can every day. I can be kept in great peace as long as I keep myself in God's love. I can enjoy keeping His commandments. Peace is the most important thing that I can have in my life. I can help teach others to follow God's law by being His witness and helping others come to know Him as their Lord and Savior. I want to be a reflection of Him and His peace.

Reflection:

Point 1. God grants me peace at any time. I can keep His peace in my heart by keeping His commandments.

Point 2. I can love obeying God's commandments and see it as an honor to help others know Him.

Point 3. I'm thankful that God never takes His peace away from me.

Prayer:

Dear Lord, thank you for allowing me to feel your peace. Help me to keep Your commandments and to be a reflection of your peace to people around me.

"*For ye shall go out with joy, and be led forth with peace...*"
Isaiah 55:22

THINGS ON MY MIND

PRAYER REQUEST

PRAYERS ANSWERED

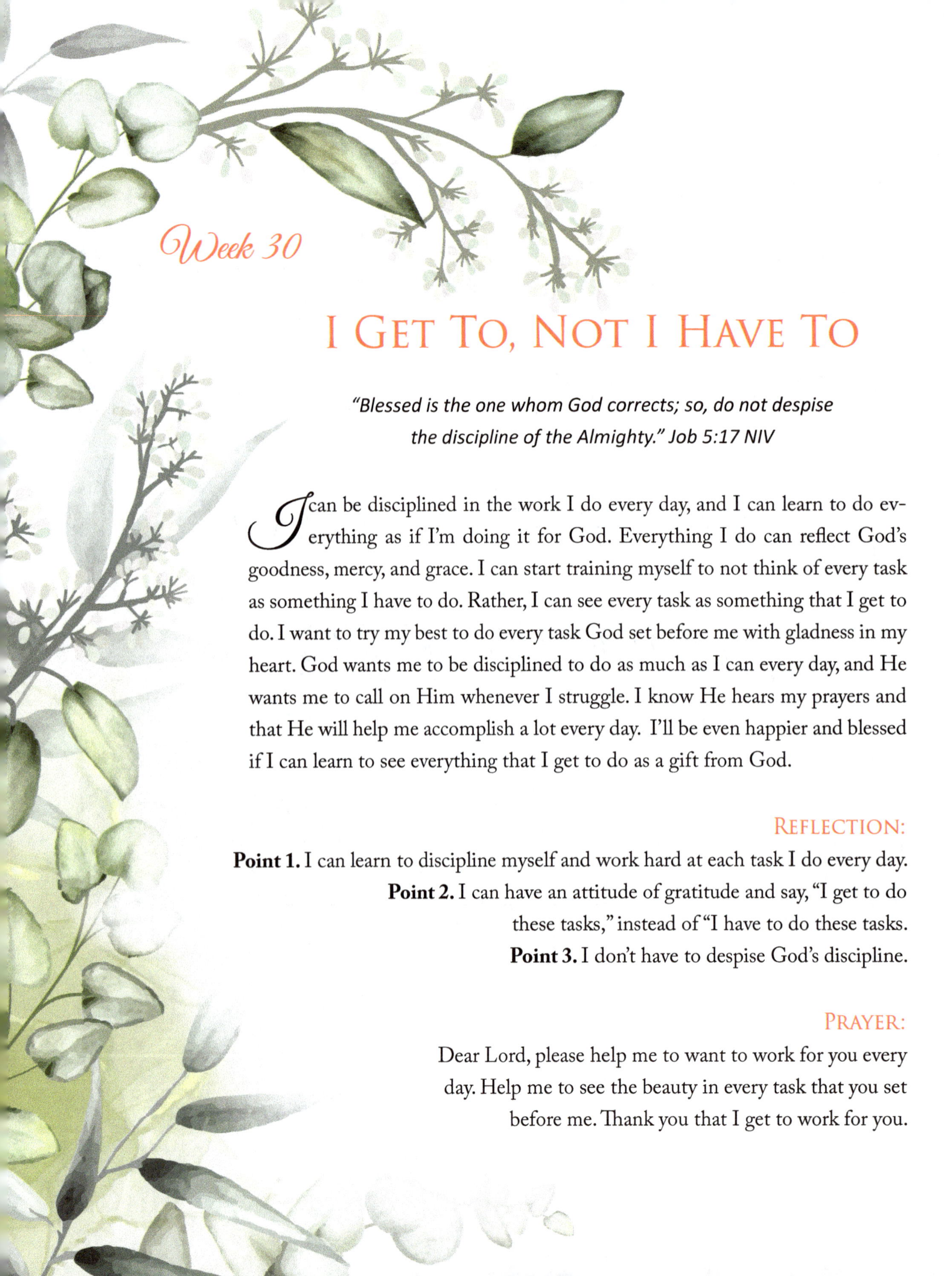

I Get To, Not I Have To

"Blessed is the one whom God corrects; so, do not despise the discipline of the Almighty." Job 5:17 NIV

I can be disciplined in the work I do every day, and I can learn to do everything as if I'm doing it for God. Everything I do can reflect God's goodness, mercy, and grace. I can start training myself to not think of every task as something I have to do. Rather, I can see every task as something that I get to do. I want to try my best to do every task God set before me with gladness in my heart. God wants me to be disciplined to do as much as I can every day, and He wants me to call on Him whenever I struggle. I know He hears my prayers and that He will help me accomplish a lot every day. I'll be even happier and blessed if I can learn to see everything that I get to do as a gift from God.

Reflection:

Point 1. I can learn to discipline myself and work hard at each task I do every day.

Point 2. I can have an attitude of gratitude and say, "I get to do these tasks," instead of "I have to do these tasks.

Point 3. I don't have to despise God's discipline.

Prayer:

Dear Lord, please help me to want to work for you every day. Help me to see the beauty in every task that you set before me. Thank you that I get to work for you.

"Your word is a lamp for my feet..." Psalm 119:105

THINGS ON MY MIND

PRAYER REQUEST

PRAYERS ANSWERED

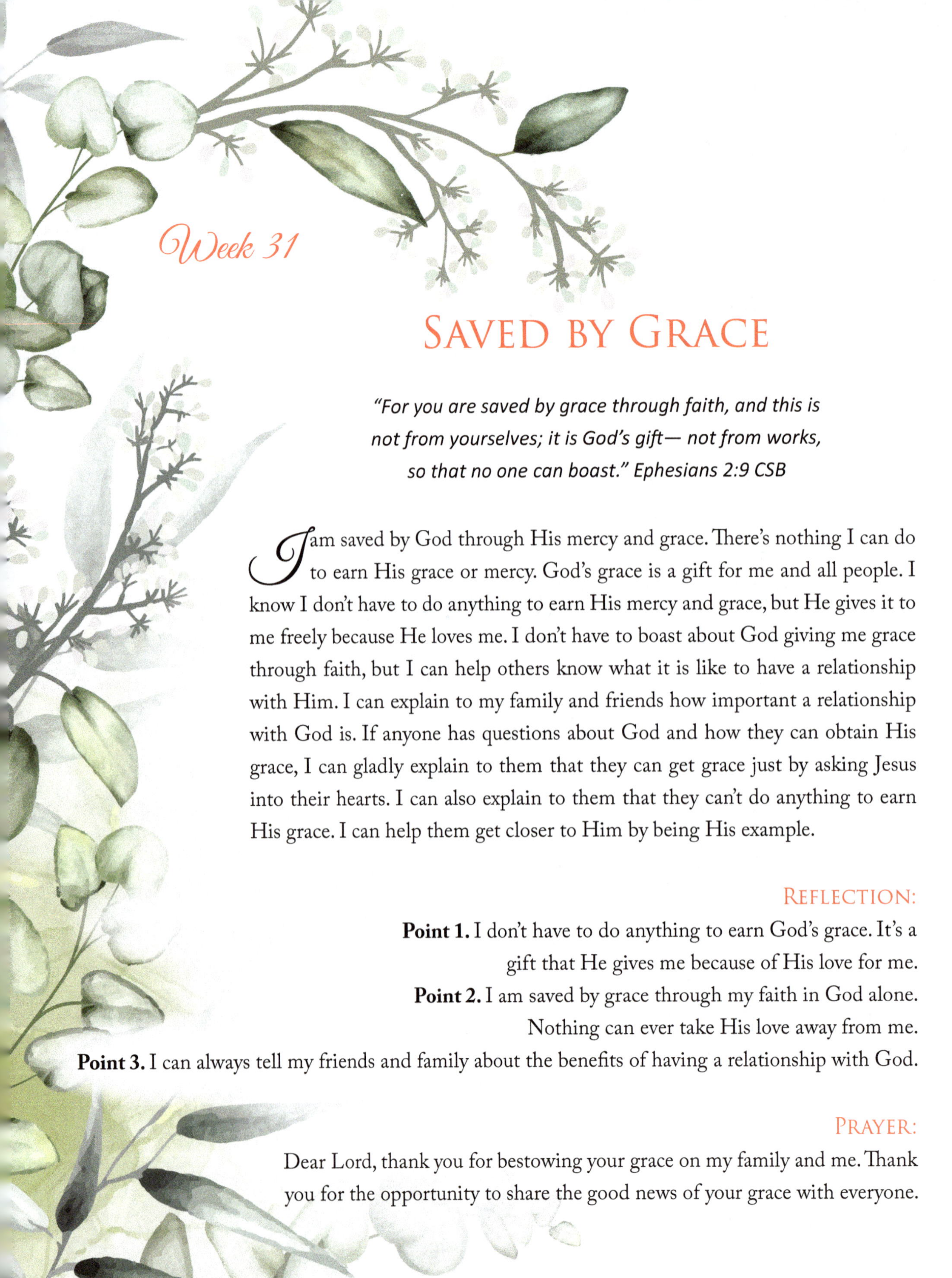

SAVED BY GRACE

"For you are saved by grace through faith, and this is not from yourselves; it is God's gift— not from works, so that no one can boast." Ephesians 2:9 CSB

I am saved by God through His mercy and grace. There's nothing I can do to earn His grace or mercy. God's grace is a gift for me and all people. I know I don't have to do anything to earn His mercy and grace, but He gives it to me freely because He loves me. I don't have to boast about God giving me grace through faith, but I can help others know what it is like to have a relationship with Him. I can explain to my family and friends how important a relationship with God is. If anyone has questions about God and how they can obtain His grace, I can gladly explain to them that they can get grace just by asking Jesus into their hearts. I can also explain to them that they can't do anything to earn His grace. I can help them get closer to Him by being His example.

REFLECTION:

Point 1. I don't have to do anything to earn God's grace. It's a gift that He gives me because of His love for me.

Point 2. I am saved by grace through my faith in God alone. Nothing can ever take His love away from me.

Point 3. I can always tell my friends and family about the benefits of having a relationship with God.

PRAYER:

Dear Lord, thank you for bestowing your grace on my family and me. Thank you for the opportunity to share the good news of your grace with everyone.

"For the grace of God has appeared, bringing salvation for all people." Titus 2:11

THINGS ON MY MIND

PRAYER REQUEST

PRAYERS ANSWERED

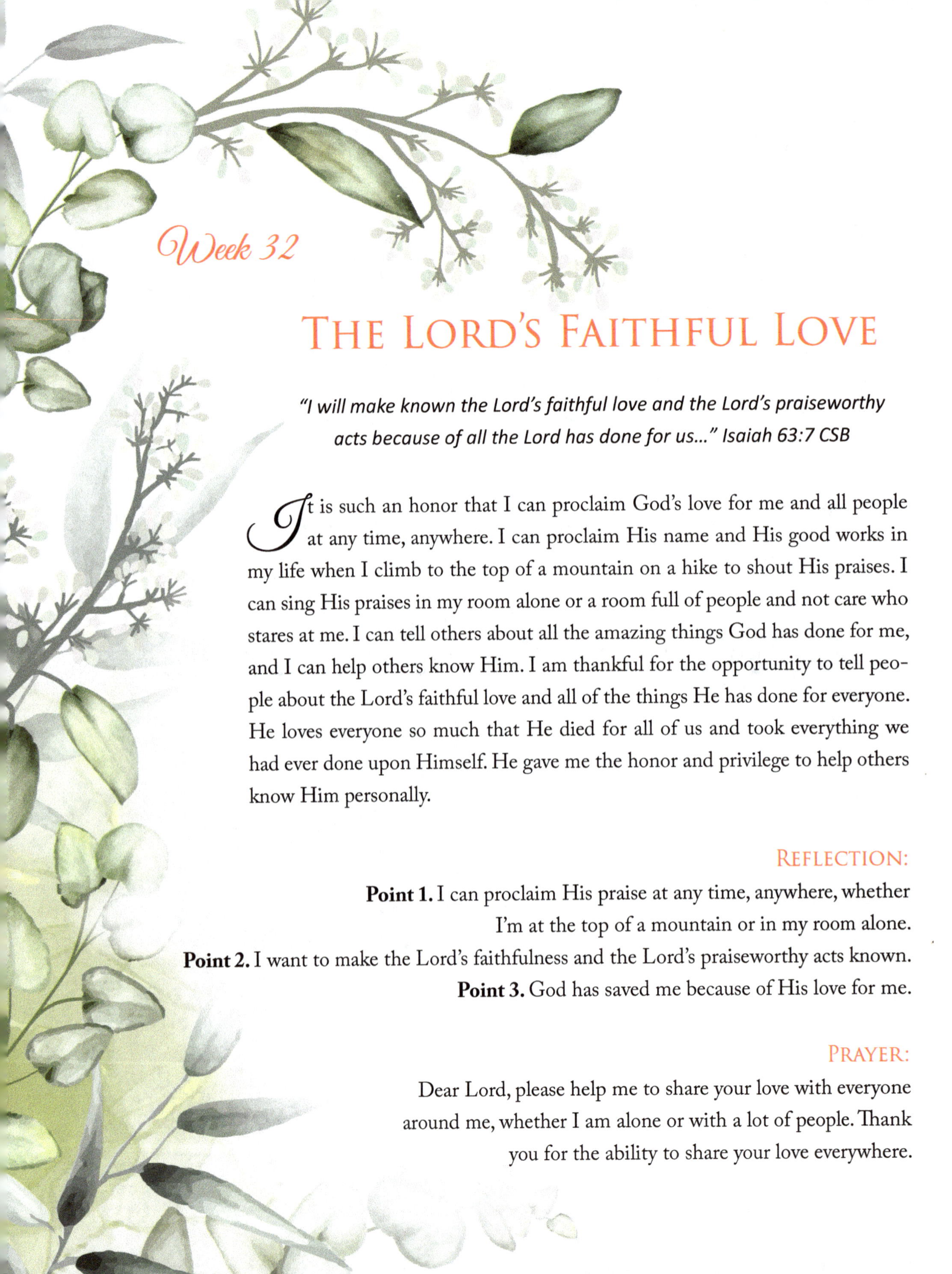

THE LORD'S FAITHFUL LOVE

"I will make known the Lord's faithful love and the Lord's praiseworthy acts because of all the Lord has done for us..." Isaiah 63:7 CSB

It is such an honor that I can proclaim God's love for me and all people at any time, anywhere. I can proclaim His name and His good works in my life when I climb to the top of a mountain on a hike to shout His praises. I can sing His praises in my room alone or a room full of people and not care who stares at me. I can tell others about all the amazing things God has done for me, and I can help others know Him. I am thankful for the opportunity to tell people about the Lord's faithful love and all of the things He has done for everyone. He loves everyone so much that He died for all of us and took everything we had ever done upon Himself. He gave me the honor and privilege to help others know Him personally.

REFLECTION:

Point 1. I can proclaim His praise at any time, anywhere, whether I'm at the top of a mountain or in my room alone.

Point 2. I want to make the Lord's faithfulness and the Lord's praiseworthy acts known.

Point 3. God has saved me because of His love for me.

PRAYER:

Dear Lord, please help me to share your love with everyone around me, whether I am alone or with a lot of people. Thank you for the ability to share your love everywhere.

"God resists the proud but gives grace to the humble."

James 4:6

THINGS ON MY MIND

PRAYER REQUEST

PRAYERS ANSWERED

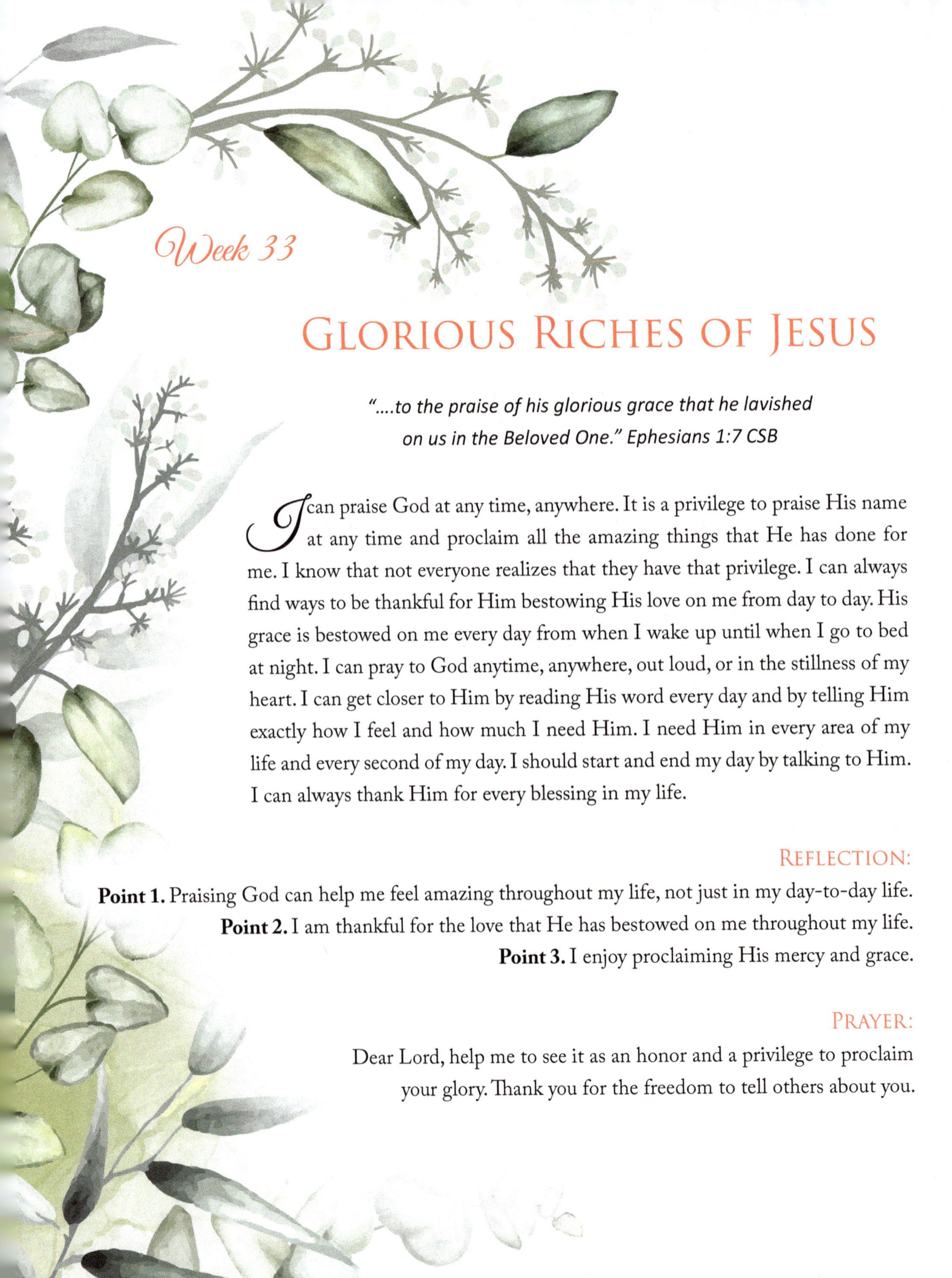

Glorious Riches of Jesus

"....to the praise of his glorious grace that he lavished on us in the Beloved One." Ephesians 1:7 CSB

I can praise God at any time, anywhere. It is a privilege to praise His name at any time and proclaim all the amazing things that He has done for me. I know that not everyone realizes that they have that privilege. I can always find ways to be thankful for Him bestowing His love on me from day to day. His grace is bestowed on me every day from when I wake up until when I go to bed at night. I can pray to God anytime, anywhere, out loud, or in the stillness of my heart. I can get closer to Him by reading His word every day and by telling Him exactly how I feel and how much I need Him. I need Him in every area of my life and every second of my day. I should start and end my day by talking to Him. I can always thank Him for every blessing in my life.

Reflection:

Point 1. Praising God can help me feel amazing throughout my life, not just in my day-to-day life.

Point 2. I am thankful for the love that He has bestowed on me throughout my life.

Point 3. I enjoy proclaiming His mercy and grace.

Prayer:

Dear Lord, help me to see it as an honor and a privilege to proclaim your glory. Thank you for the freedom to tell others about you.

"Indeed, we have all received grace upon grace..." John 1:16

THINGS ON MY MIND

PRAYER REQUEST

PRAYERS ANSWERED

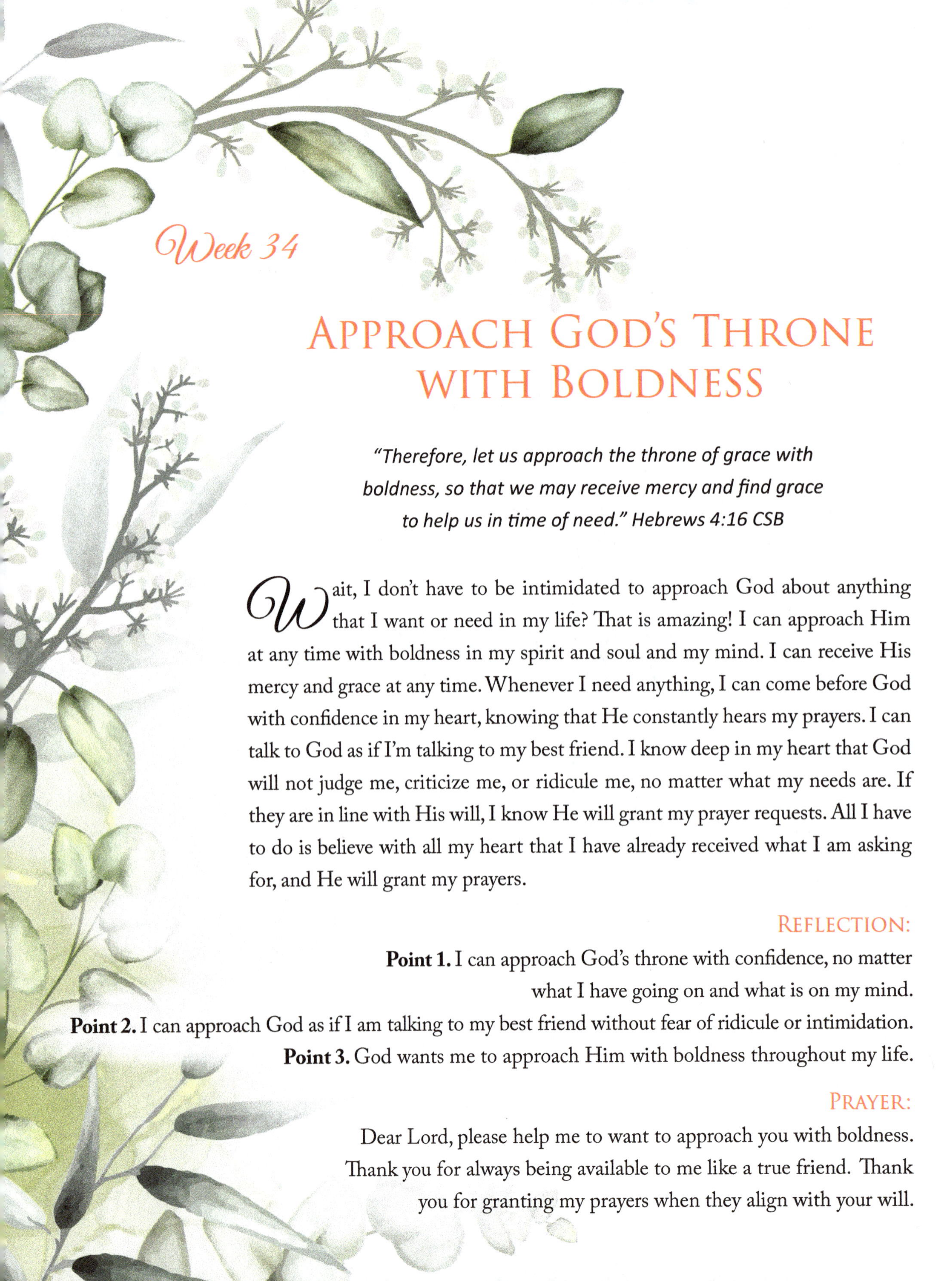

Approach God's Throne with Boldness

"Therefore, let us approach the throne of grace with boldness, so that we may receive mercy and find grace to help us in time of need." Hebrews 4:16 CSB

Wait, I don't have to be intimidated to approach God about anything that I want or need in my life? That is amazing! I can approach Him at any time with boldness in my spirit and soul and my mind. I can receive His mercy and grace at any time. Whenever I need anything, I can come before God with confidence in my heart, knowing that He constantly hears my prayers. I can talk to God as if I'm talking to my best friend. I know deep in my heart that God will not judge me, criticize me, or ridicule me, no matter what my needs are. If they are in line with His will, I know He will grant my prayer requests. All I have to do is believe with all my heart that I have already received what I am asking for, and He will grant my prayers.

REFLECTION:

Point 1. I can approach God's throne with confidence, no matter what I have going on and what is on my mind.

Point 2. I can approach God as if I am talking to my best friend without fear of ridicule or intimidation.

Point 3. God wants me to approach Him with boldness throughout my life.

PRAYER:

Dear Lord, please help me to want to approach you with boldness. Thank you for always being available to me like a true friend. Thank you for granting my prayers when they align with your will.

"The Lord is compassionate and gracious..." Psalm 103:8

THINGS ON MY MIND

PRAYER REQUEST

PRAYERS ANSWERED

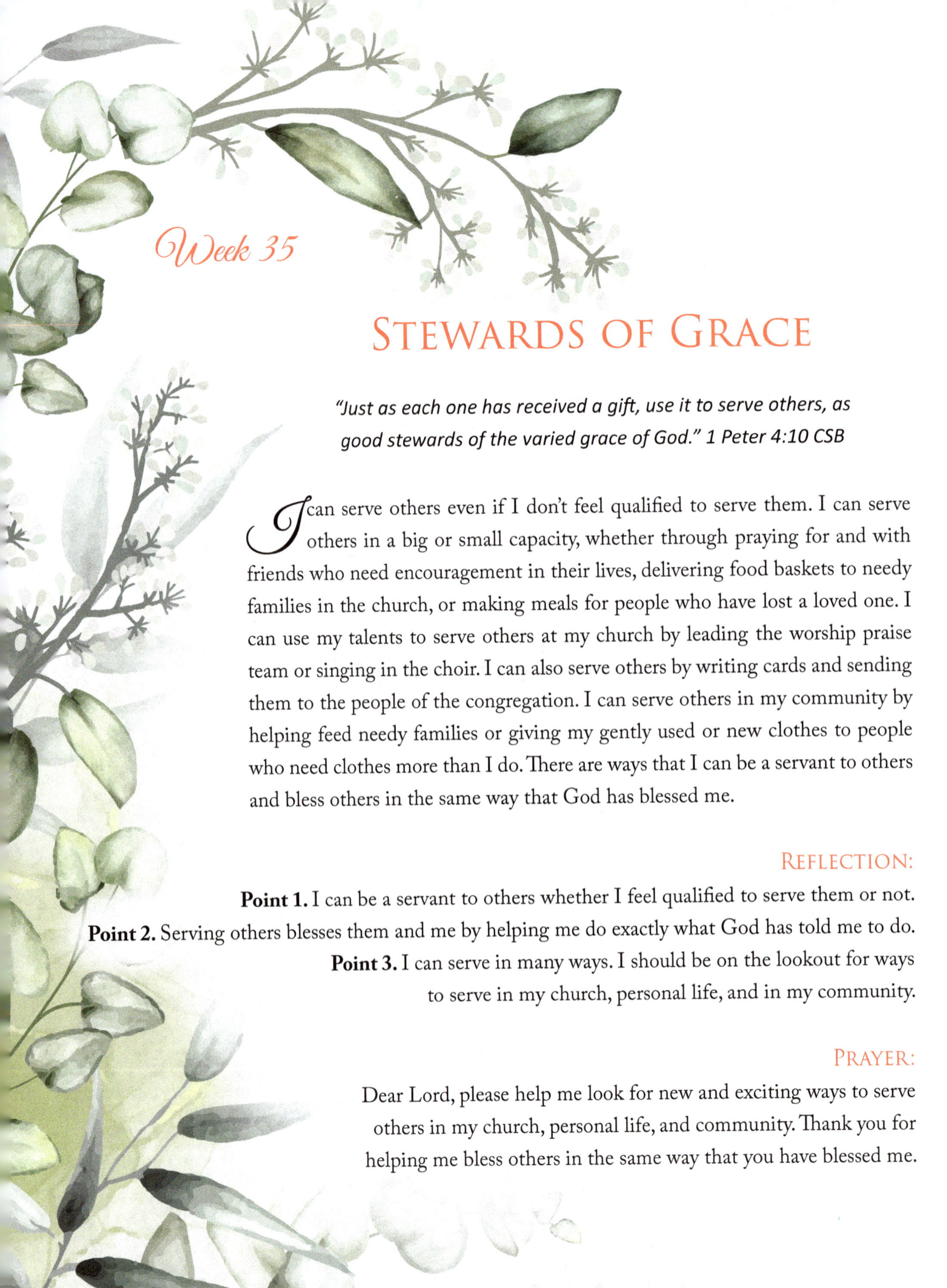

STEWARDS OF GRACE

"Just as each one has received a gift, use it to serve others, as good stewards of the varied grace of God." 1 Peter 4:10 CSB

I can serve others even if I don't feel qualified to serve them. I can serve others in a big or small capacity, whether through praying for and with friends who need encouragement in their lives, delivering food baskets to needy families in the church, or making meals for people who have lost a loved one. I can use my talents to serve others at my church by leading the worship praise team or singing in the choir. I can also serve others by writing cards and sending them to the people of the congregation. I can serve others in my community by helping feed needy families or giving my gently used or new clothes to people who need clothes more than I do. There are ways that I can be a servant to others and bless others in the same way that God has blessed me.

REFLECTION:

Point 1. I can be a servant to others whether I feel qualified to serve them or not.

Point 2. Serving others blesses them and me by helping me do exactly what God has told me to do.

Point 3. I can serve in many ways. I should be on the lookout for ways to serve in my church, personal life, and in my community.

PRAYER:

Dear Lord, please help me look for new and exciting ways to serve others in my church, personal life, and community. Thank you for helping me bless others in the same way that you have blessed me.

"Therefore, the Lord is waiting to show you mercy..." Isaiah 30:18

Things on My Mind

Prayer Request

Prayers Answered

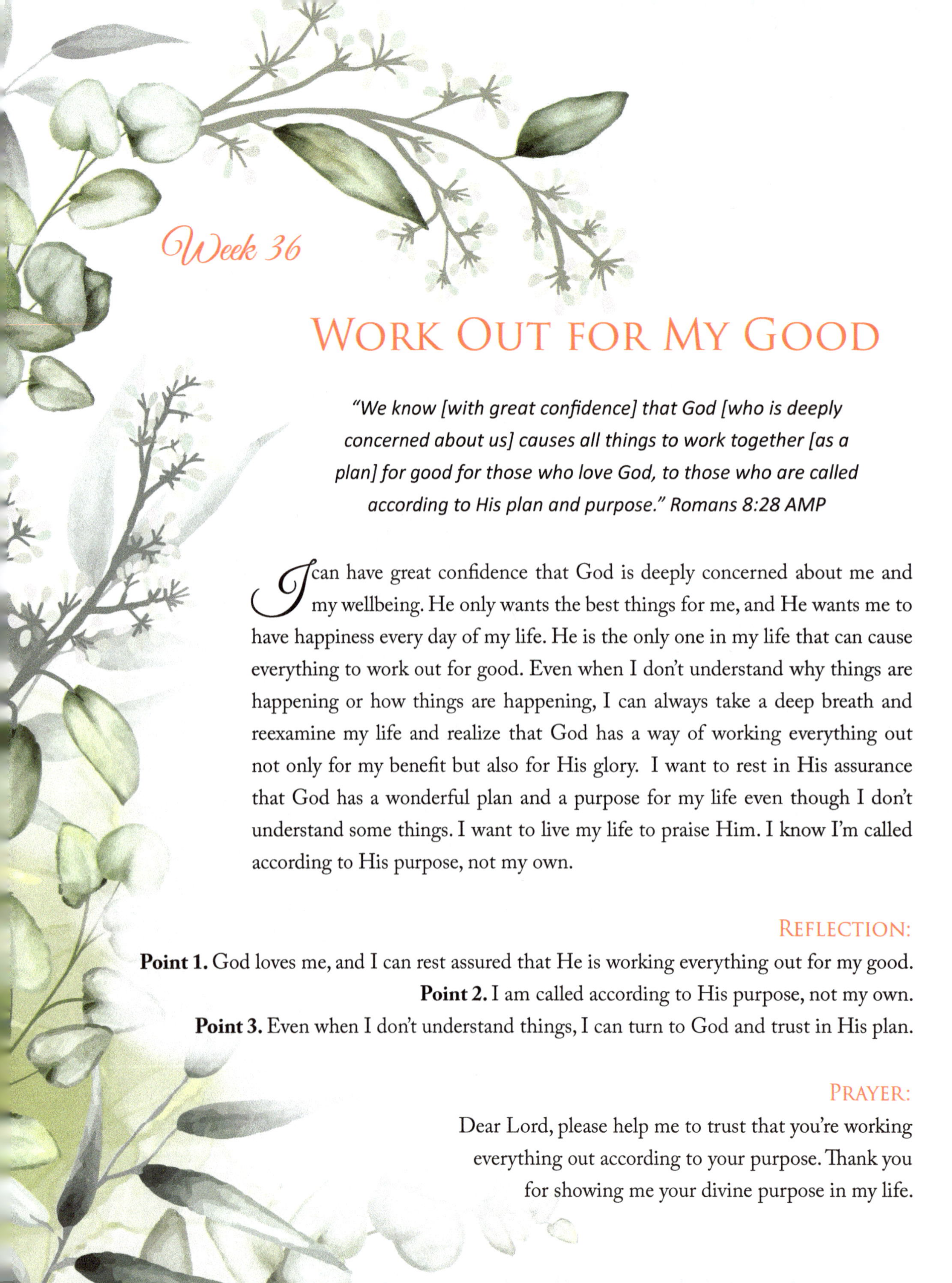

Work Out for My Good

"We know [with great confidence] that God [who is deeply concerned about us] causes all things to work together [as a plan] for good for those who love God, to those who are called according to His plan and purpose." Romans 8:28 AMP

I can have great confidence that God is deeply concerned about me and my wellbeing. He only wants the best things for me, and He wants me to have happiness every day of my life. He is the only one in my life that can cause everything to work out for good. Even when I don't understand why things are happening or how things are happening, I can always take a deep breath and reexamine my life and realize that God has a way of working everything out not only for my benefit but also for His glory. I want to rest in His assurance that God has a wonderful plan and a purpose for my life even though I don't understand some things. I want to live my life to praise Him. I know I'm called according to His purpose, not my own.

Reflection:

Point 1. God loves me, and I can rest assured that He is working everything out for my good.

Point 2. I am called according to His purpose, not my own.

Point 3. Even when I don't understand things, I can turn to God and trust in His plan.

Prayer:

Dear Lord, please help me to trust that you're working everything out according to your purpose. Thank you for showing me your divine purpose in my life.

"He has made everything beautiful in its time."
Ecclesiastes 3:11

THINGS ON MY MIND

PRAYER REQUEST

PRAYERS ANSWERED

The Day the Lord Has Made

"This [day in which God has saved me] is the day which the Lord has made; Let us rejoice and be glad in it." Psalm 118:24 AMP

God gives me new and exciting opportunities to follow Him every day. When I wake up, I should see it as a blessing and learn to enjoy every minute that I have to serve Him. There is always something to be thankful for each day. Sometimes I can just be thankful for the fact that God even woke me up. When God gives me another day to live, it means that His purpose for me on this earth isn't finished yet. Every day I must use my gifts and talents to bring others to Christ and help others know Him as their personal Lord and Savior. God has saved me every day in more ways than one, and I need to take the time every day to think about how He has saved me. I can rejoice and be glad in my everyday life, thanks to God.

Reflection:

Point 1. Every day I can be thankful for another day of life.
Point 2. Every day God has saved me time and time again. I can always reflect on what He has done for me.
Point 3. I can rejoice that God gave me another day of life to be a witness for Him.

Prayer:

Dear Lord, please help me to see every day as a precious gift from you. Thank you that I can enjoy every day on earth and be glad that you gave me another day of life.

"For without him, who can eat or find enjoyment?" Ecclesiastes 2:25

THINGS ON MY MIND

PRAYER REQUEST

PRAYERS ANSWERED

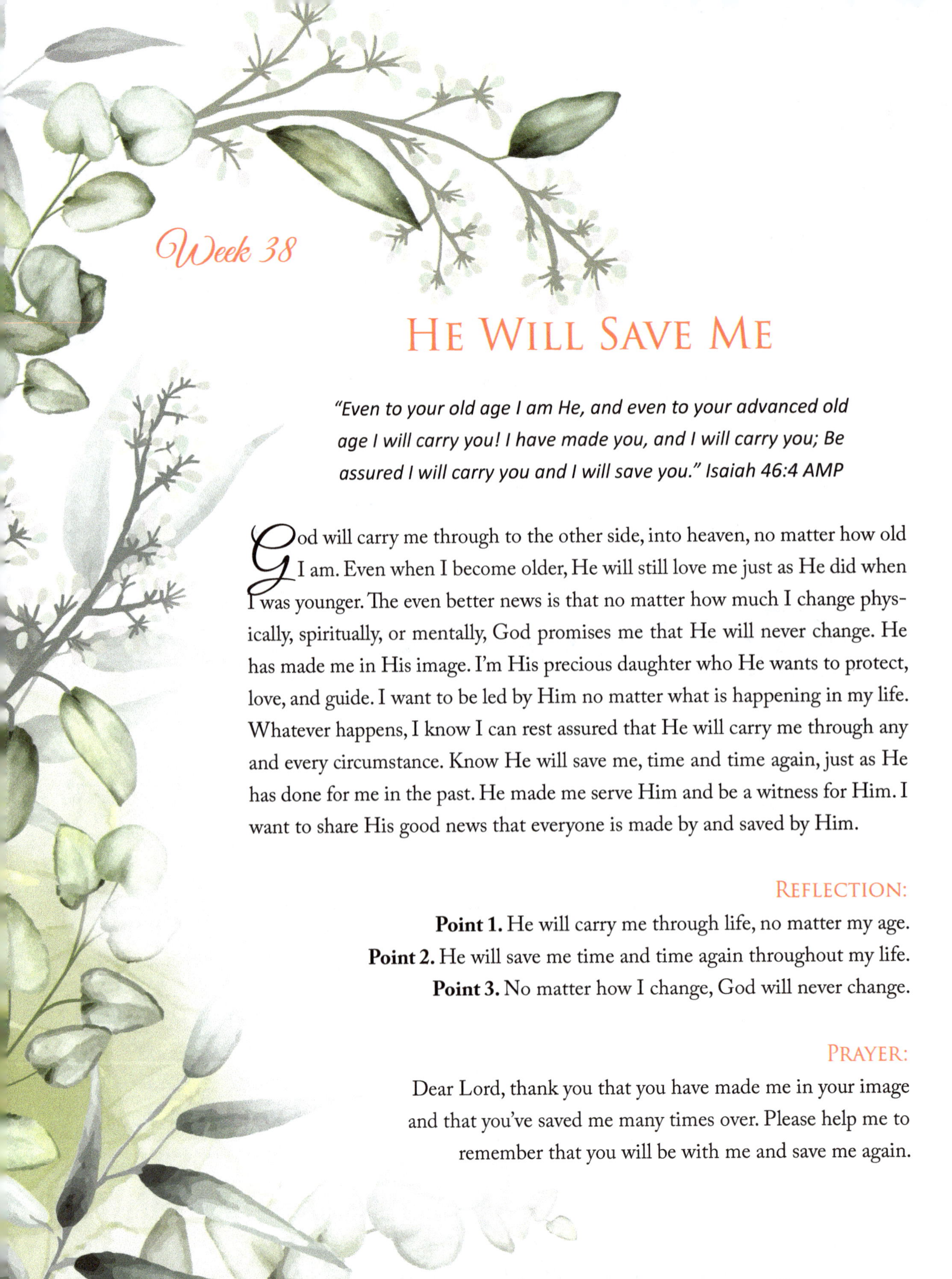

He Will Save Me

"Even to your old age I am He, and even to your advanced old age I will carry you! I have made you, and I will carry you; Be assured I will carry you and I will save you." Isaiah 46:4 AMP

God will carry me through to the other side, into heaven, no matter how old I am. Even when I become older, He will still love me just as He did when I was younger. The even better news is that no matter how much I change physically, spiritually, or mentally, God promises me that He will never change. He has made me in His image. I'm His precious daughter who He wants to protect, love, and guide. I want to be led by Him no matter what is happening in my life. Whatever happens, I know I can rest assured that He will carry me through any and every circumstance. Know He will save me, time and time again, just as He has done for me in the past. He made me serve Him and be a witness for Him. I want to share His good news that everyone is made by and saved by Him.

Reflection:

Point 1. He will carry me through life, no matter my age.
Point 2. He will save me time and time again throughout my life.
Point 3. No matter how I change, God will never change.

Prayer:

Dear Lord, thank you that you have made me in your image and that you've saved me many times over. Please help me to remember that you will be with me and save me again.

"Do not be conformed to this world." Romans 12:2

THINGS ON MY MIND

PRAYER REQUEST

PRAYERS ANSWERED

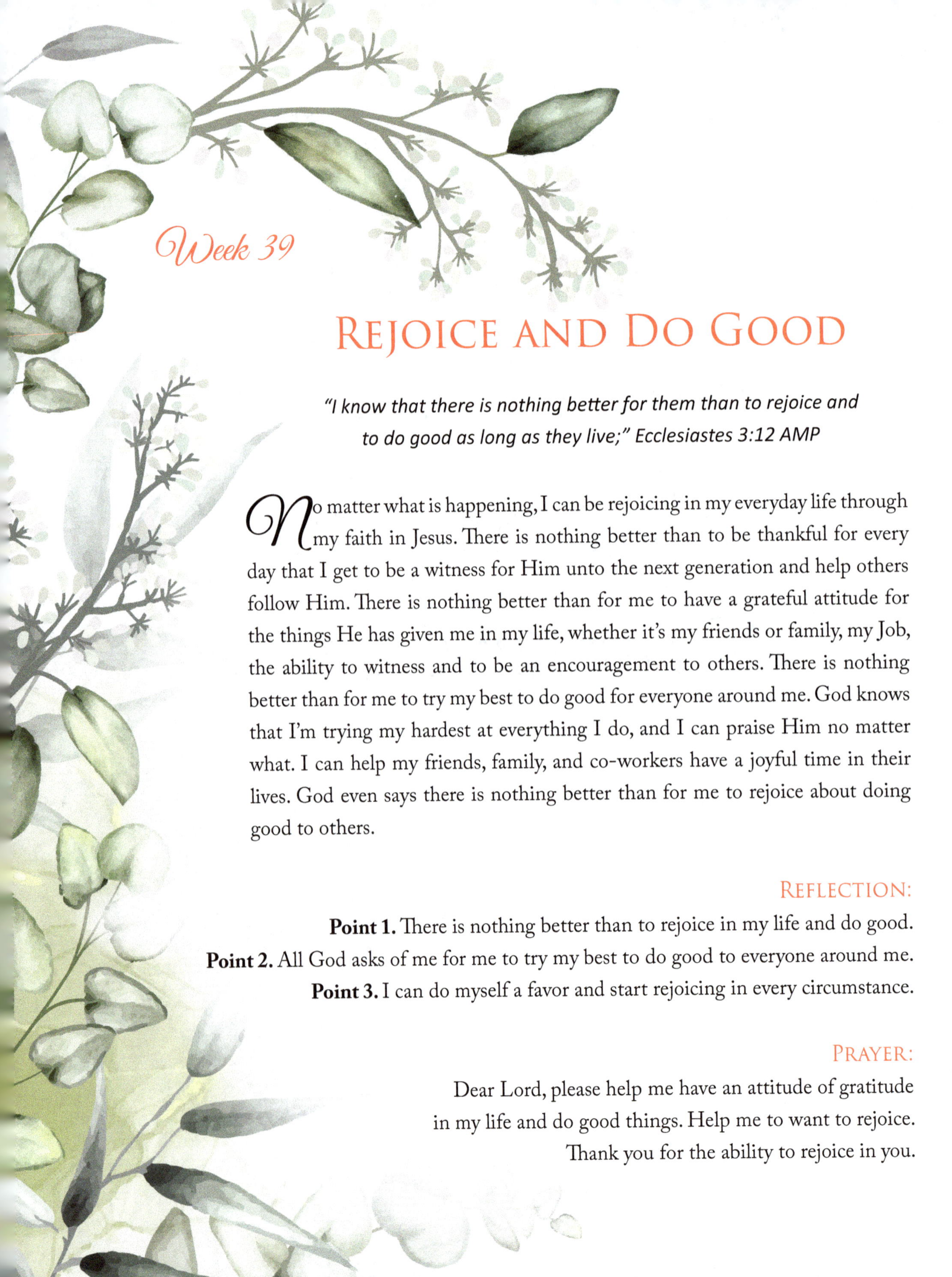

Rejoice and Do Good

"I know that there is nothing better for them than to rejoice and to do good as long as they live;" Ecclesiastes 3:12 AMP

No matter what is happening, I can be rejoicing in my everyday life through my faith in Jesus. There is nothing better than to be thankful for every day that I get to be a witness for Him unto the next generation and help others follow Him. There is nothing better than for me to have a grateful attitude for the things He has given me in my life, whether it's my friends or family, my Job, the ability to witness and to be an encouragement to others. There is nothing better than for me to try my best to do good for everyone around me. God knows that I'm trying my hardest at everything I do, and I can praise Him no matter what. I can help my friends, family, and co-workers have a joyful time in their lives. God even says there is nothing better than for me to rejoice about doing good to others.

Reflection:

Point 1. There is nothing better than to rejoice in my life and do good.

Point 2. All God asks of me for me to try my best to do good to everyone around me.

Point 3. I can do myself a favor and start rejoicing in every circumstance.

Prayer:

Dear Lord, please help me have an attitude of gratitude in my life and do good things. Help me to want to rejoice. Thank you for the ability to rejoice in you.

"Good judgment wins favor..." Proverbs 15:13

THINGS ON MY MIND

PRAYER REQUEST

PRAYERS ANSWERED

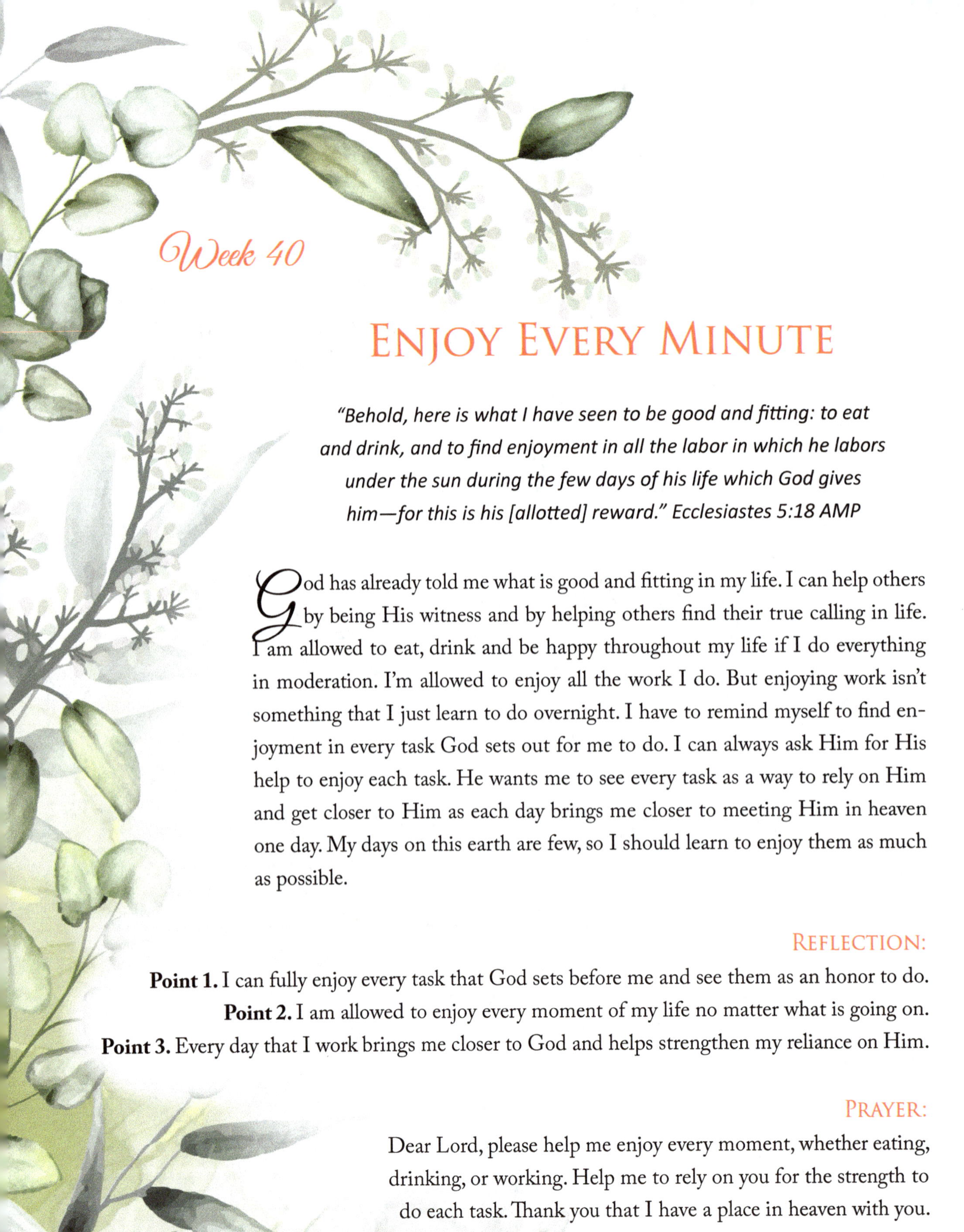

Enjoy Every Minute

"Behold, here is what I have seen to be good and fitting: to eat and drink, and to find enjoyment in all the labor in which he labors under the sun during the few days of his life which God gives him—for this is his [allotted] reward." Ecclesiastes 5:18 AMP

God has already told me what is good and fitting in my life. I can help others by being His witness and by helping others find their true calling in life. I am allowed to eat, drink and be happy throughout my life if I do everything in moderation. I'm allowed to enjoy all the work I do. But enjoying work isn't something that I just learn to do overnight. I have to remind myself to find enjoyment in every task God sets out for me to do. I can always ask Him for His help to enjoy each task. He wants me to see every task as a way to rely on Him and get closer to Him as each day brings me closer to meeting Him in heaven one day. My days on this earth are few, so I should learn to enjoy them as much as possible.

REFLECTION:

Point 1. I can fully enjoy every task that God sets before me and see them as an honor to do.

Point 2. I am allowed to enjoy every moment of my life no matter what is going on.

Point 3. Every day that I work brings me closer to God and helps strengthen my reliance on Him.

PRAYER:

Dear Lord, please help me enjoy every moment, whether eating, drinking, or working. Help me to rely on you for the strength to do each task. Thank you that I have a place in heaven with you.

"A heart at peace gives life to the body."

Proverbs 14:30

THINGS ON MY MIND

PRAYER REQUEST

PRAYERS ANSWERED

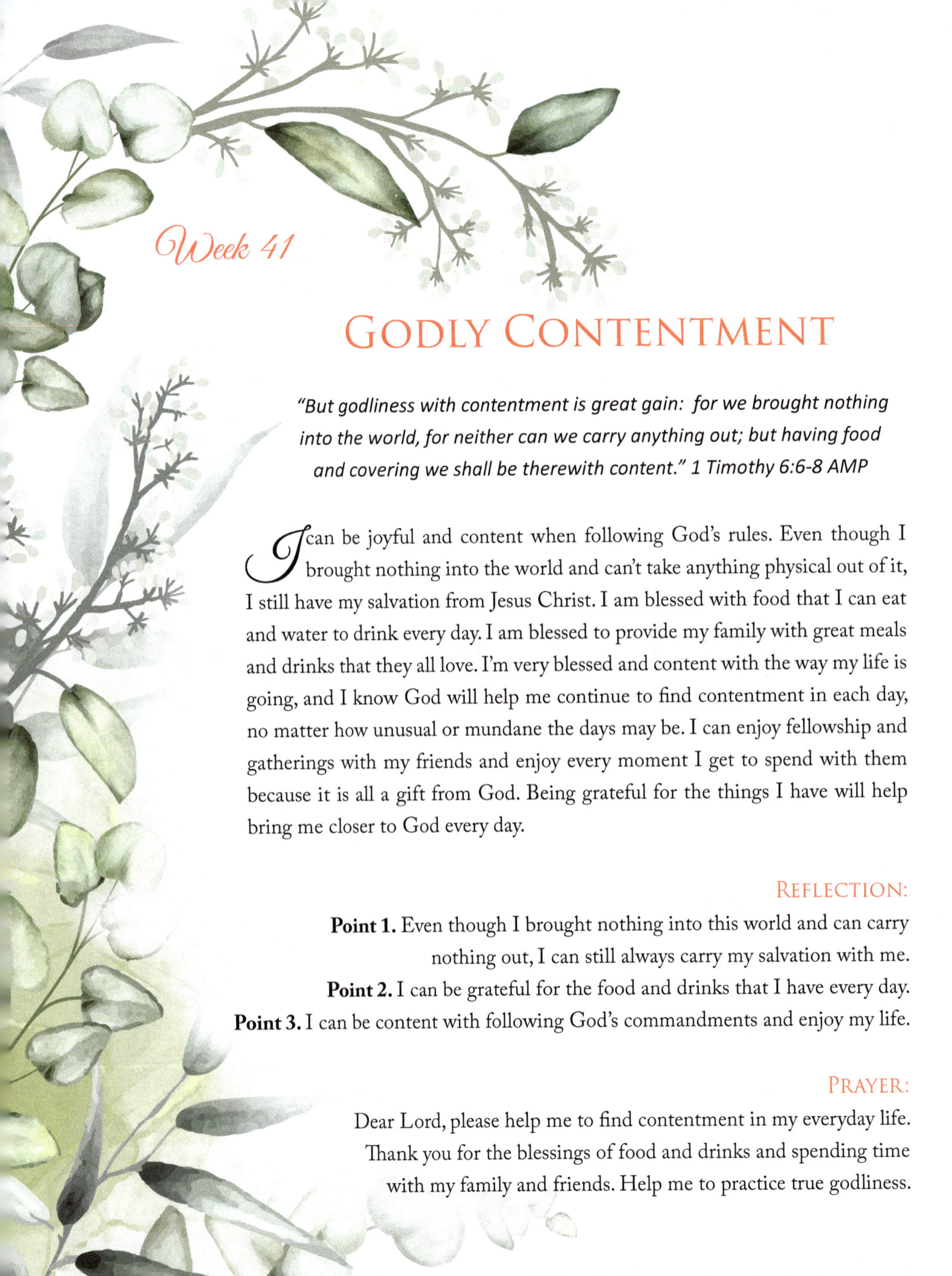

Godly Contentment

"But godliness with contentment is great gain: for we brought nothing into the world, for neither can we carry anything out; but having food and covering we shall be therewith content." 1 Timothy 6:6-8 AMP

I can be joyful and content when following God's rules. Even though I brought nothing into the world and can't take anything physical out of it, I still have my salvation from Jesus Christ. I am blessed with food that I can eat and water to drink every day. I am blessed to provide my family with great meals and drinks that they all love. I'm very blessed and content with the way my life is going, and I know God will help me continue to find contentment in each day, no matter how unusual or mundane the days may be. I can enjoy fellowship and gatherings with my friends and enjoy every moment I get to spend with them because it is all a gift from God. Being grateful for the things I have will help bring me closer to God every day.

Reflection:

Point 1. Even though I brought nothing into this world and can carry nothing out, I can still always carry my salvation with me.
Point 2. I can be grateful for the food and drinks that I have every day.
Point 3. I can be content with following God's commandments and enjoy my life.

Prayer:

Dear Lord, please help me to find contentment in my everyday life. Thank you for the blessings of food and drinks and spending time with my family and friends. Help me to practice true godliness.

"...they will spend the rest of their days in prosperity..."
Job 36:11

THINGS ON MY MIND

PRAYER REQUEST

PRAYERS ANSWERED

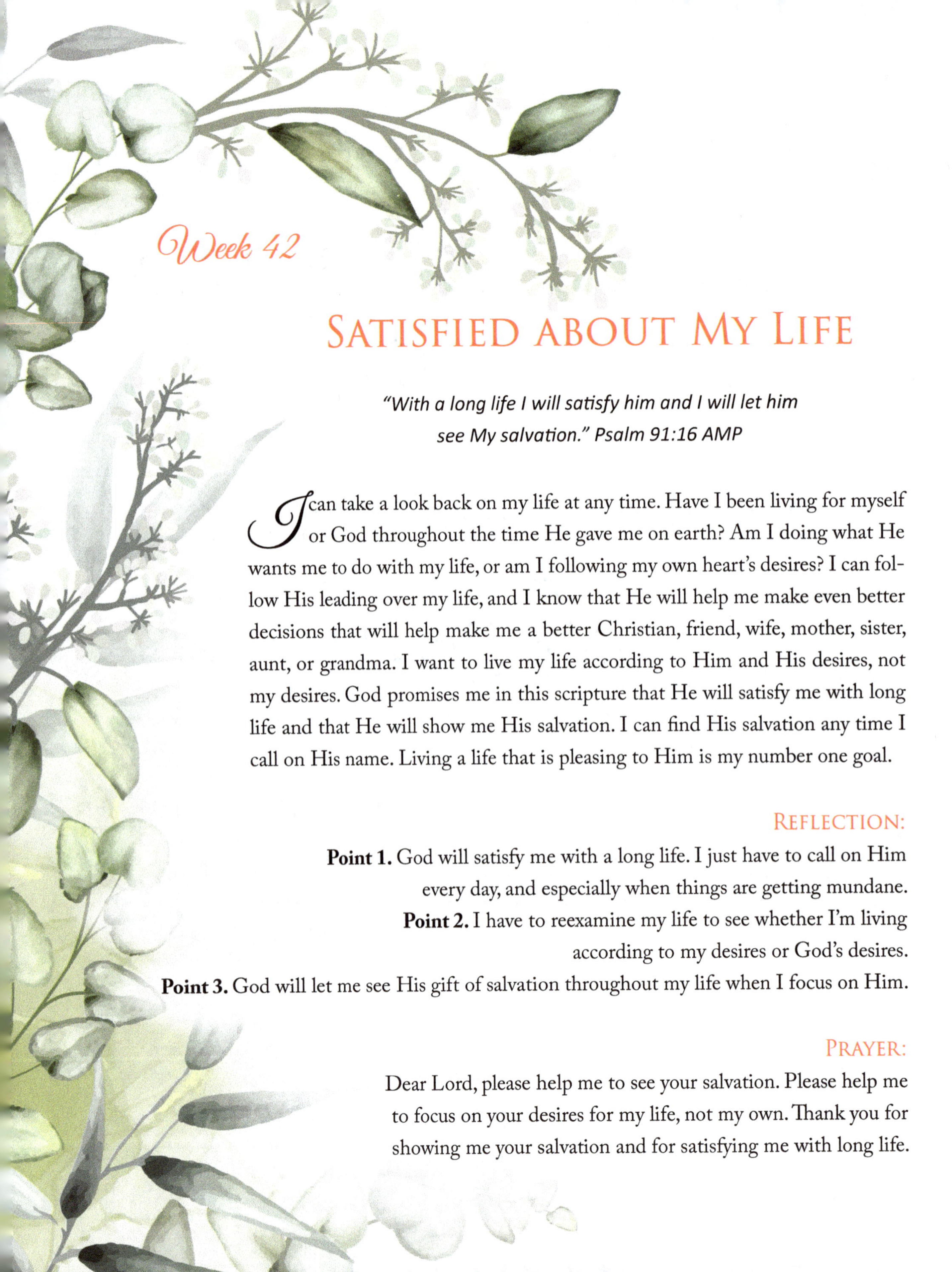

Satisfied about My Life

*"With a long life I will satisfy him and I will let him
see My salvation." Psalm 91:16 AMP*

I can take a look back on my life at any time. Have I been living for myself or God throughout the time He gave me on earth? Am I doing what He wants me to do with my life, or am I following my own heart's desires? I can follow His leading over my life, and I know that He will help me make even better decisions that will help make me a better Christian, friend, wife, mother, sister, aunt, or grandma. I want to live my life according to Him and His desires, not my desires. God promises me in this scripture that He will satisfy me with long life and that He will show me His salvation. I can find His salvation any time I call on His name. Living a life that is pleasing to Him is my number one goal.

Reflection:

Point 1. God will satisfy me with a long life. I just have to call on Him every day, and especially when things are getting mundane.

Point 2. I have to reexamine my life to see whether I'm living according to my desires or God's desires.

Point 3. God will let me see His gift of salvation throughout my life when I focus on Him.

Prayer:

Dear Lord, please help me to see your salvation. Please help me to focus on your desires for my life, not my own. Thank you for showing me your salvation and for satisfying me with long life.

"Commit your way to the Lord..." Psalm 37:5

THINGS ON MY MIND

PRAYER REQUEST

PRAYERS ANSWERED

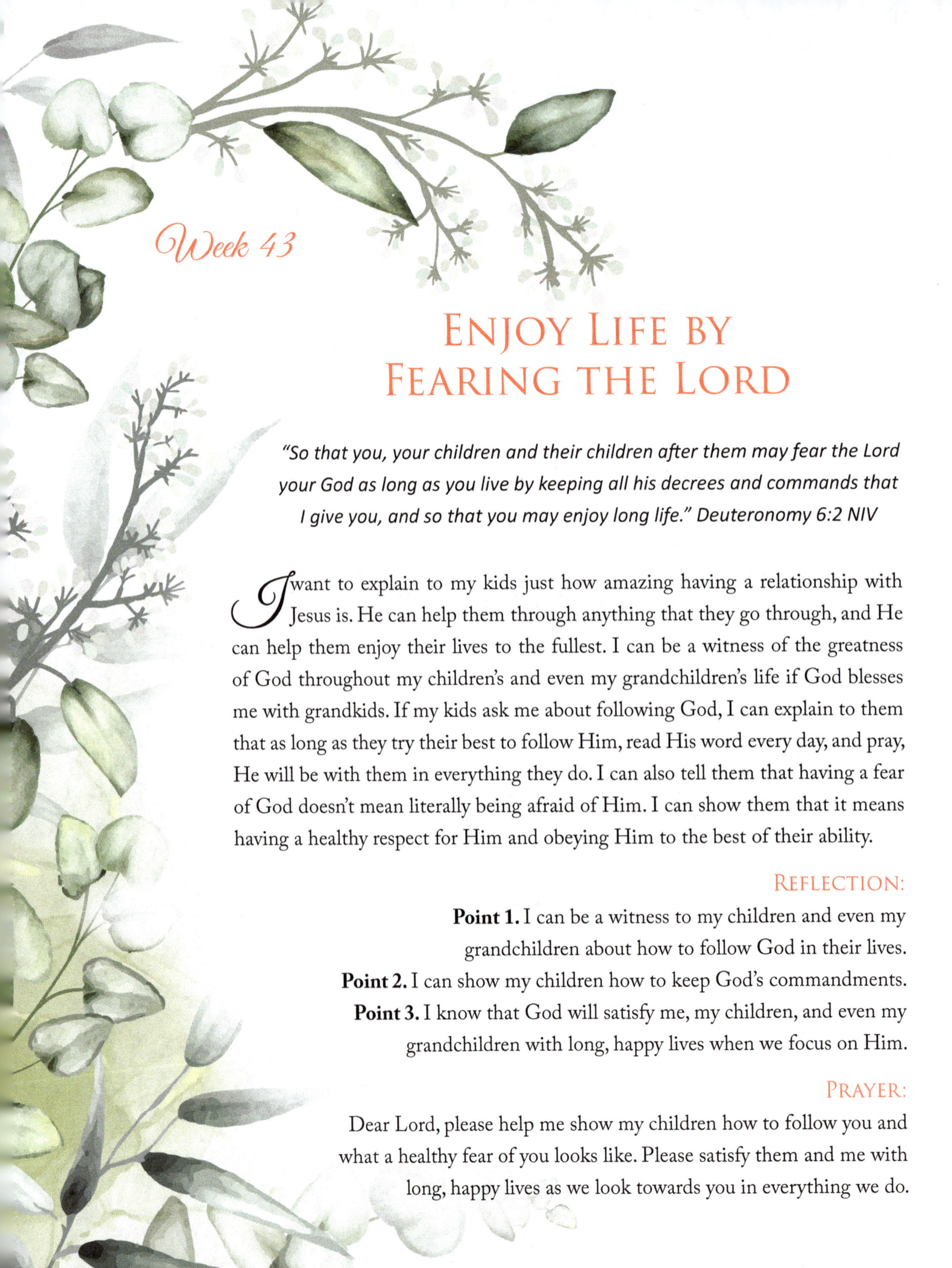

Enjoy Life by Fearing the Lord

"So that you, your children and their children after them may fear the Lord your God as long as you live by keeping all his decrees and commands that I give you, and so that you may enjoy long life." Deuteronomy 6:2 NIV

I want to explain to my kids just how amazing having a relationship with Jesus is. He can help them through anything that they go through, and He can help them enjoy their lives to the fullest. I can be a witness of the greatness of God throughout my children's and even my grandchildren's life if God blesses me with grandkids. If my kids ask me about following God, I can explain to them that as long as they try their best to follow Him, read His word every day, and pray, He will be with them in everything they do. I can also tell them that having a fear of God doesn't mean literally being afraid of Him. I can show them that it means having a healthy respect for Him and obeying Him to the best of their ability.

REFLECTION:

Point 1. I can be a witness to my children and even my grandchildren about how to follow God in their lives.

Point 2. I can show my children how to keep God's commandments.

Point 3. I know that God will satisfy me, my children, and even my grandchildren with long, happy lives when we focus on Him.

PRAYER:

Dear Lord, please help me show my children how to follow you and what a healthy fear of you looks like. Please satisfy them and me with long, happy lives as we look towards you in everything we do.

"'Long life to you! Good health to you and your household!'" 1 Samuel 25:6

THINGS ON MY MIND

PRAYER REQUEST

PRAYERS ANSWERED

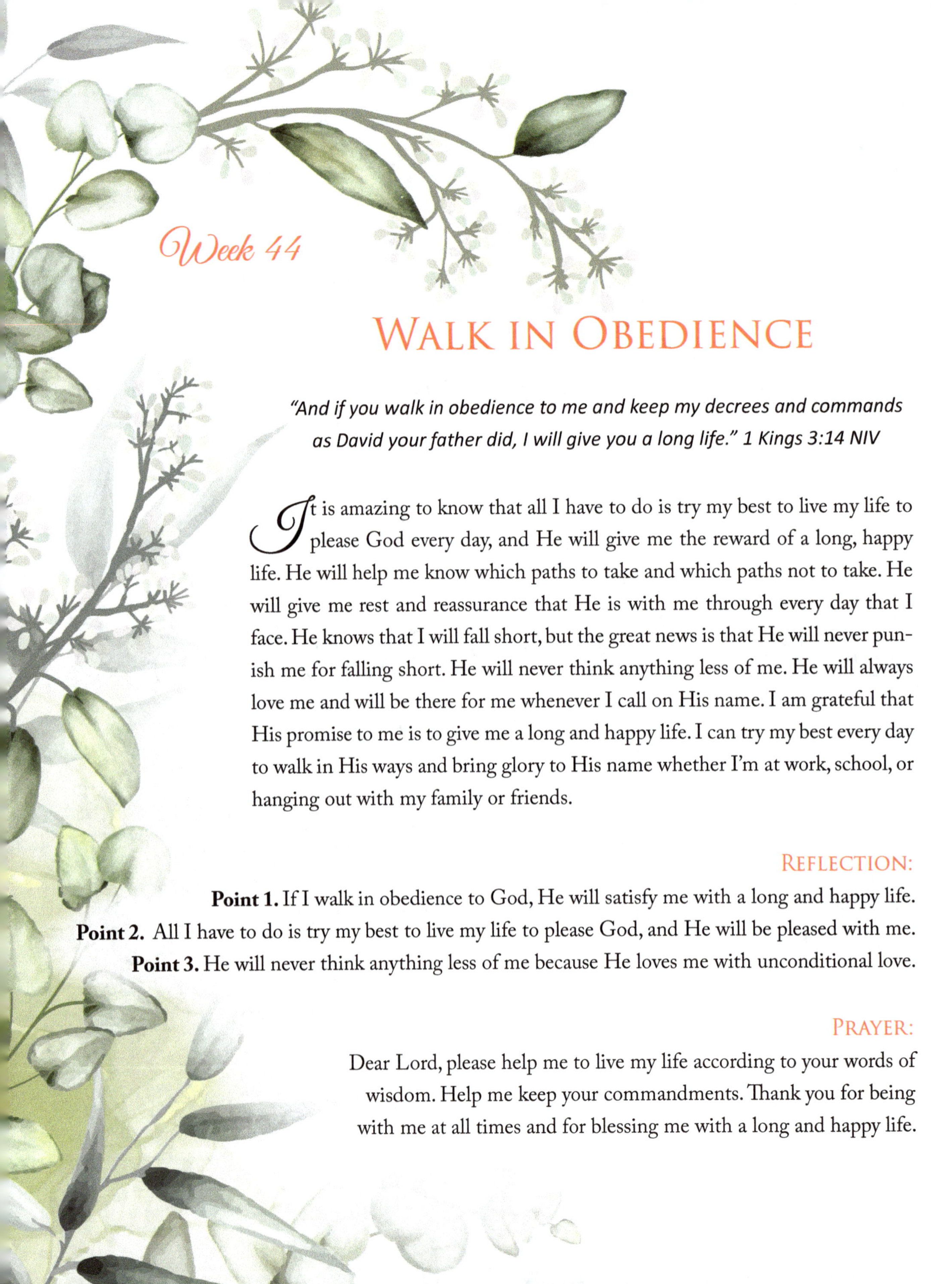

Walk in Obedience

"And if you walk in obedience to me and keep my decrees and commands as David your father did, I will give you a long life." 1 Kings 3:14 NIV

It is amazing to know that all I have to do is try my best to live my life to please God every day, and He will give me the reward of a long, happy life. He will help me know which paths to take and which paths not to take. He will give me rest and reassurance that He is with me through every day that I face. He knows that I will fall short, but the great news is that He will never punish me for falling short. He will never think anything less of me. He will always love me and will be there for me whenever I call on His name. I am grateful that His promise to me is to give me a long and happy life. I can try my best every day to walk in His ways and bring glory to His name whether I'm at work, school, or hanging out with my family or friends.

Reflection:

Point 1. If I walk in obedience to God, He will satisfy me with a long and happy life.
Point 2. All I have to do is try my best to live my life to please God, and He will be pleased with me.
Point 3. He will never think anything less of me because He loves me with unconditional love.

Prayer:

Dear Lord, please help me to live my life according to your words of wisdom. Help me keep your commandments. Thank you for being with me at all times and for blessing me with a long and happy life.

"...Does not long life bring understanding?"
Job 12:12

THINGS ON MY MIND

PRAYER REQUEST

PRAYERS ANSWERED

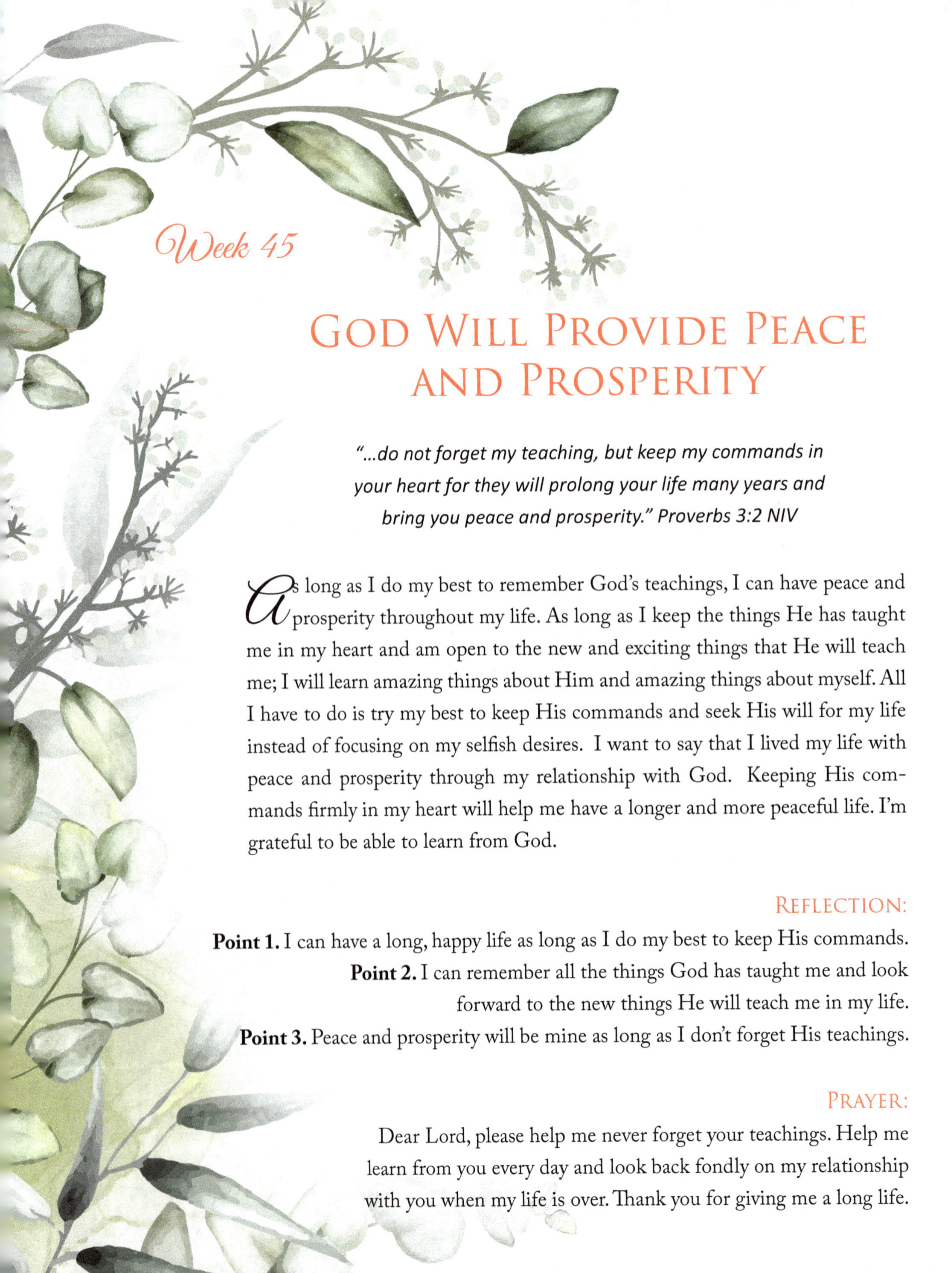

God Will Provide Peace and Prosperity

"...do not forget my teaching, but keep my commands in your heart for they will prolong your life many years and bring you peace and prosperity." Proverbs 3:2 NIV

As long as I do my best to remember God's teachings, I can have peace and prosperity throughout my life. As long as I keep the things He has taught me in my heart and am open to the new and exciting things that He will teach me; I will learn amazing things about Him and amazing things about myself. All I have to do is try my best to keep His commands and seek His will for my life instead of focusing on my selfish desires. I want to say that I lived my life with peace and prosperity through my relationship with God. Keeping His commands firmly in my heart will help me have a longer and more peaceful life. I'm grateful to be able to learn from God.

Reflection:

Point 1. I can have a long, happy life as long as I do my best to keep His commands.

Point 2. I can remember all the things God has taught me and look forward to the new things He will teach me in my life.

Point 3. Peace and prosperity will be mine as long as I don't forget His teachings.

Prayer:

Dear Lord, please help me never forget your teachings. Help me learn from you every day and look back fondly on my relationship with you when my life is over. Thank you for giving me a long life.

"For he himself is our peace... Ephesians 2:14

THINGS ON MY MIND

PRAYER REQUEST

PRAYERS ANSWERED

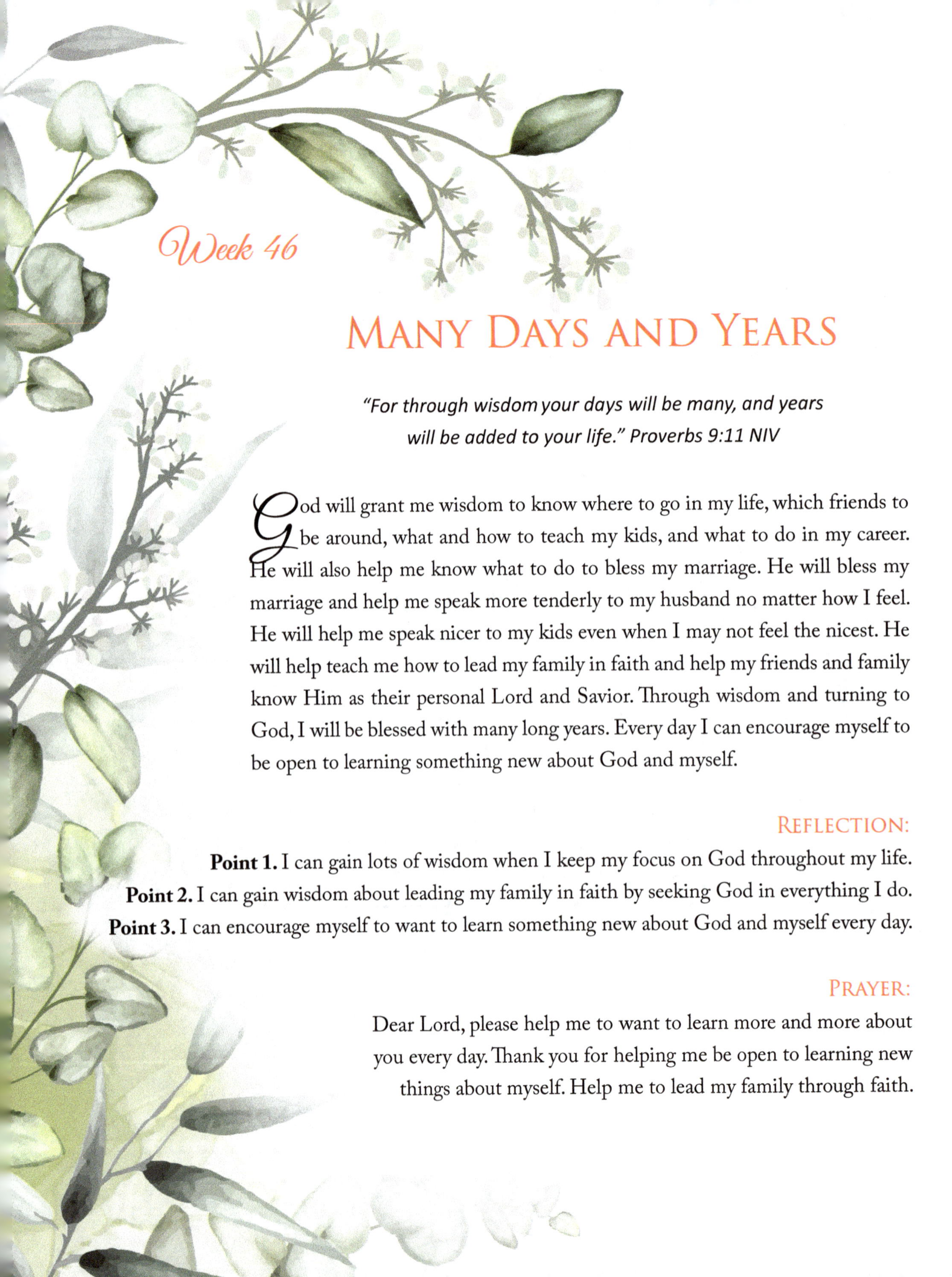

Many Days and Years

"For through wisdom your days will be many, and years will be added to your life." Proverbs 9:11 NIV

God will grant me wisdom to know where to go in my life, which friends to be around, what and how to teach my kids, and what to do in my career. He will also help me know what to do to bless my marriage. He will bless my marriage and help me speak more tenderly to my husband no matter how I feel. He will help me speak nicer to my kids even when I may not feel the nicest. He will help teach me how to lead my family in faith and help my friends and family know Him as their personal Lord and Savior. Through wisdom and turning to God, I will be blessed with many long years. Every day I can encourage myself to be open to learning something new about God and myself.

REFLECTION:

Point 1. I can gain lots of wisdom when I keep my focus on God throughout my life.
Point 2. I can gain wisdom about leading my family in faith by seeking God in everything I do.
Point 3. I can encourage myself to want to learn something new about God and myself every day.

PRAYER:

Dear Lord, please help me to want to learn more and more about you every day. Thank you for helping me be open to learning new things about myself. Help me to lead my family through faith.

"The fear of the Lord adds length to life..." Proverbs 10:27

THINGS ON MY MIND

PRAYER REQUEST

PRAYERS ANSWERED

Rest in the Shadow of the Almighty

"He who dwells in the shelter of the Most High will abide in the shadow of the Almighty. I will say to the Lord, "My refuge and my fortress, my God, in whom I trust." Psalm 91:1-2 NIV

I can talk about God at every moment of my life without fear. I can encourage my friends or family members to go to God whenever they need a faith boost. Whenever I dwell in the secret place of the most high, I can rest in God's almighty shadow and know that He is keeping me safe and spiritually secure. God wants to be my fortress and the person in whom I trust the most because He will never let me down or fail me. He will never stop loving me with His unconditional love and mercy. His grace follows me everywhere I go. He is my refuge, and I can cling to Him. I can rest in His arms at any time and find the peace and reassurance that I've been longing for. I can turn to Him for peace, comfort, and restoration.

Reflection:

Point 1. I can dwell in His secret place at any time and know that He is always with me.

Point 2. God can restore my peace and comfort whenever I call on Him.

Point 3. I can rest in the shadow of God and find peace and contentment.

Prayer:

Dear Lord, thank you for allowing me to come before you at any time for peace, contentment, and restoration. Please help me to guide others to you in everything I say and do.

"Everyone who lives and believes in me shall never die..." John 11:26

THINGS ON MY MIND

PRAYER REQUEST

PRAYERS ANSWERED

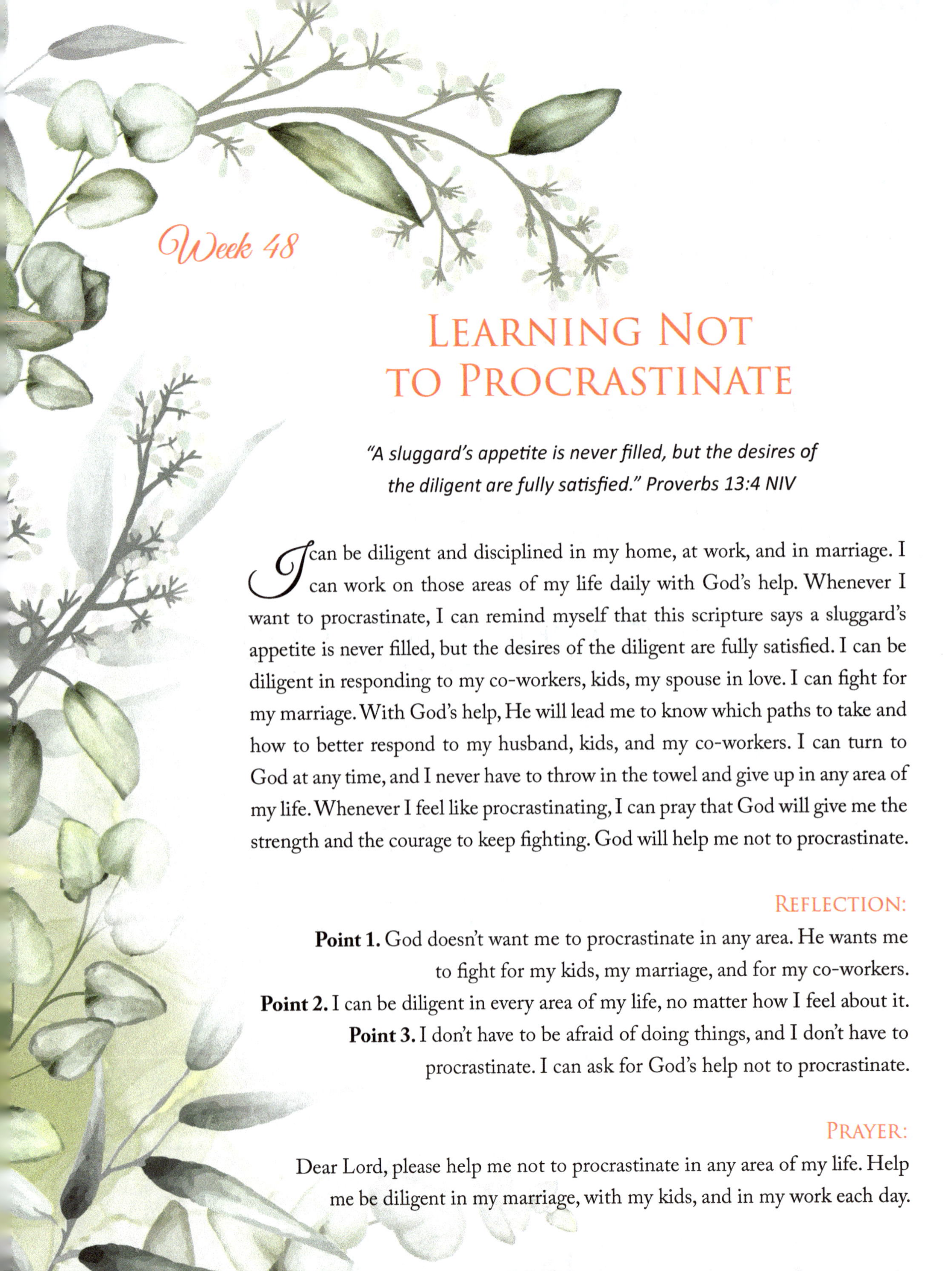

Learning Not to Procrastinate

*"A sluggard's appetite is never filled, but the desires of
the diligent are fully satisfied." Proverbs 13:4 NIV*

I can be diligent and disciplined in my home, at work, and in marriage. I can work on those areas of my life daily with God's help. Whenever I want to procrastinate, I can remind myself that this scripture says a sluggard's appetite is never filled, but the desires of the diligent are fully satisfied. I can be diligent in responding to my co-workers, kids, my spouse in love. I can fight for my marriage. With God's help, He will lead me to know which paths to take and how to better respond to my husband, kids, and my co-workers. I can turn to God at any time, and I never have to throw in the towel and give up in any area of my life. Whenever I feel like procrastinating, I can pray that God will give me the strength and the courage to keep fighting. God will help me not to procrastinate.

Reflection:

Point 1. God doesn't want me to procrastinate in any area. He wants me to fight for my kids, my marriage, and for my co-workers.

Point 2. I can be diligent in every area of my life, no matter how I feel about it.

Point 3. I don't have to be afraid of doing things, and I don't have to procrastinate. I can ask for God's help not to procrastinate.

Prayer:

Dear Lord, please help me not to procrastinate in any area of my life. Help me be diligent in my marriage, with my kids, and in my work each day.

"...make the most of every opportunity."
Colossians 4:5

THINGS ON MY MIND

PRAYER REQUEST

PRAYERS ANSWERED

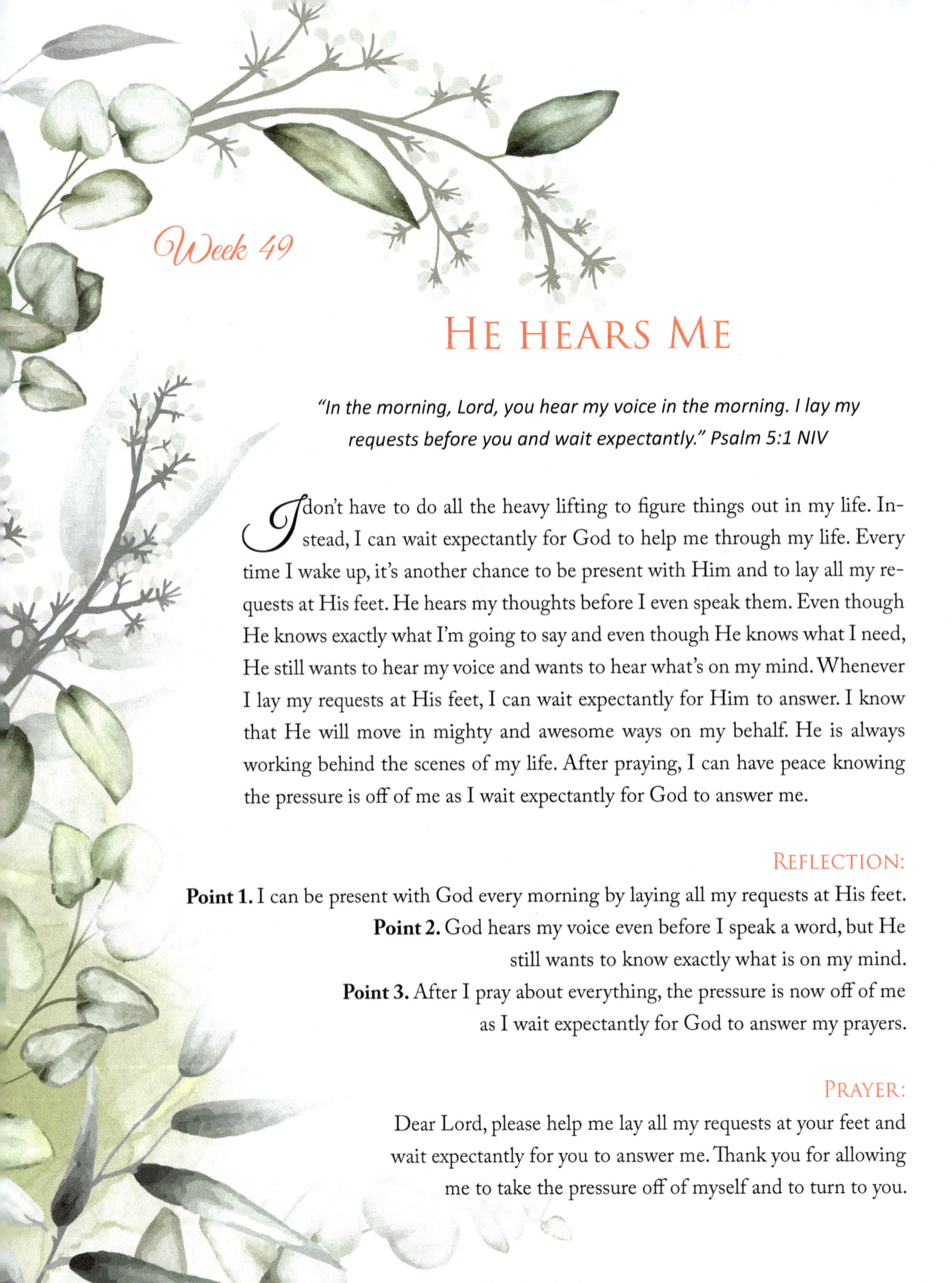

He hears Me

"In the morning, Lord, you hear my voice in the morning. I lay my requests before you and wait expectantly." Psalm 5:1 NIV

I don't have to do all the heavy lifting to figure things out in my life. Instead, I can wait expectantly for God to help me through my life. Every time I wake up, it's another chance to be present with Him and to lay all my requests at His feet. He hears my thoughts before I even speak them. Even though He knows exactly what I'm going to say and even though He knows what I need, He still wants to hear my voice and wants to hear what's on my mind. Whenever I lay my requests at His feet, I can wait expectantly for Him to answer. I know that He will move in mighty and awesome ways on my behalf. He is always working behind the scenes of my life. After praying, I can have peace knowing the pressure is off of me as I wait expectantly for God to answer me.

Reflection:

Point 1. I can be present with God every morning by laying all my requests at His feet.

Point 2. God hears my voice even before I speak a word, but He still wants to know exactly what is on my mind.

Point 3. After I pray about everything, the pressure is now off of me as I wait expectantly for God to answer my prayers.

Prayer:

Dear Lord, please help me lay all my requests at your feet and wait expectantly for you to answer me. Thank you for allowing me to take the pressure off of myself and to turn to you.

"When he calls to me, I will answer him." Psalm 91:14

THINGS ON MY MIND

PRAYER REQUEST

PRAYERS ANSWERED

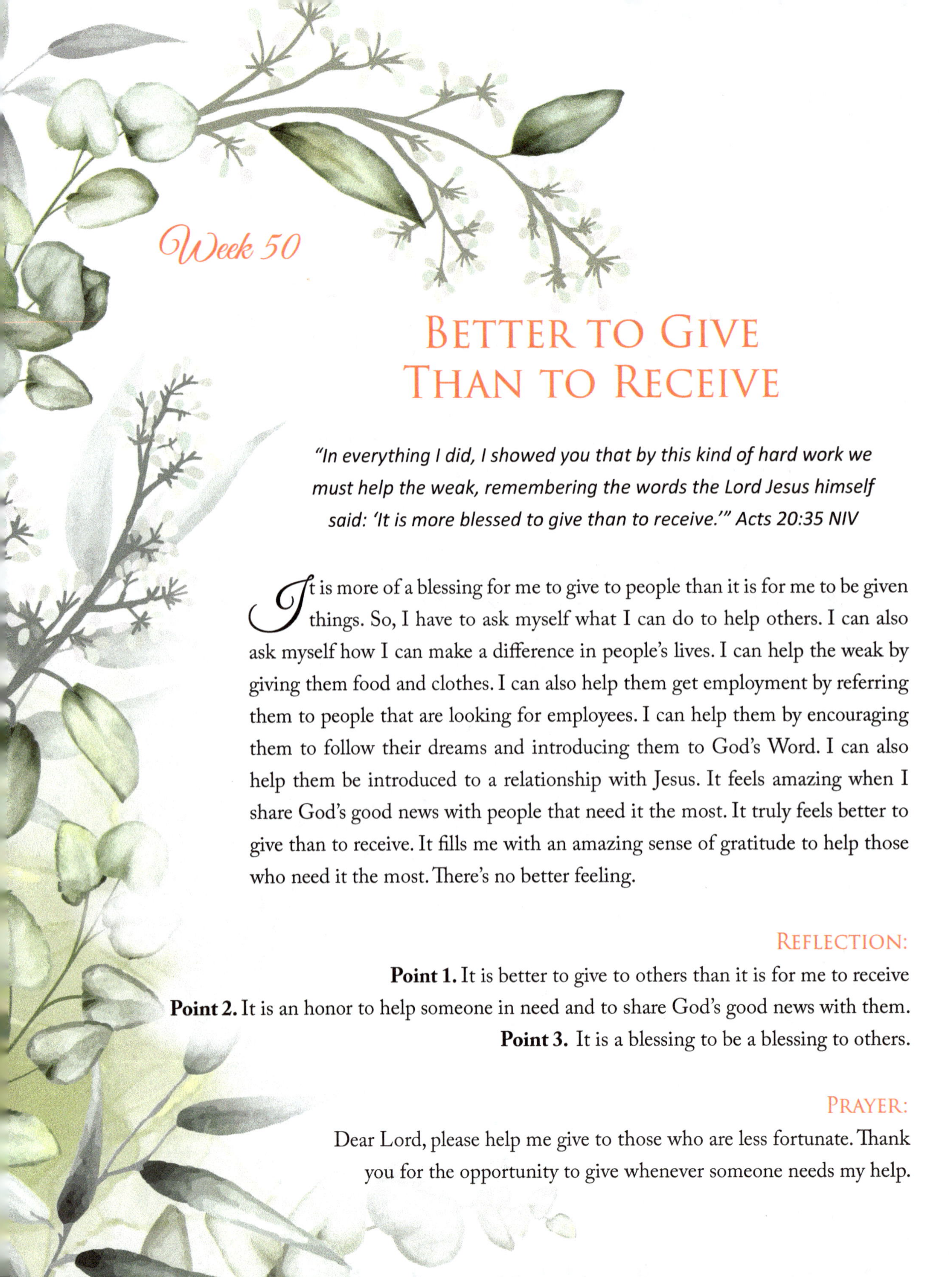

Better to Give Than to Receive

"In everything I did, I showed you that by this kind of hard work we must help the weak, remembering the words the Lord Jesus himself said: 'It is more blessed to give than to receive.'" Acts 20:35 NIV

It is more of a blessing for me to give to people than it is for me to be given things. So, I have to ask myself what I can do to help others. I can also ask myself how I can make a difference in people's lives. I can help the weak by giving them food and clothes. I can also help them get employment by referring them to people that are looking for employees. I can help them by encouraging them to follow their dreams and introducing them to God's Word. I can also help them be introduced to a relationship with Jesus. It feels amazing when I share God's good news with people that need it the most. It truly feels better to give than to receive. It fills me with an amazing sense of gratitude to help those who need it the most. There's no better feeling.

Reflection:

Point 1. It is better to give to others than it is for me to receive

Point 2. It is an honor to help someone in need and to share God's good news with them.

Point 3. It is a blessing to be a blessing to others.

Prayer:

Dear Lord, please help me give to those who are less fortunate. Thank you for the opportunity to give whenever someone needs my help.

"A joyful heart is good medicine." Proverbs 17:22

THINGS ON MY MIND

PRAYER REQUEST

PRAYERS ANSWERED

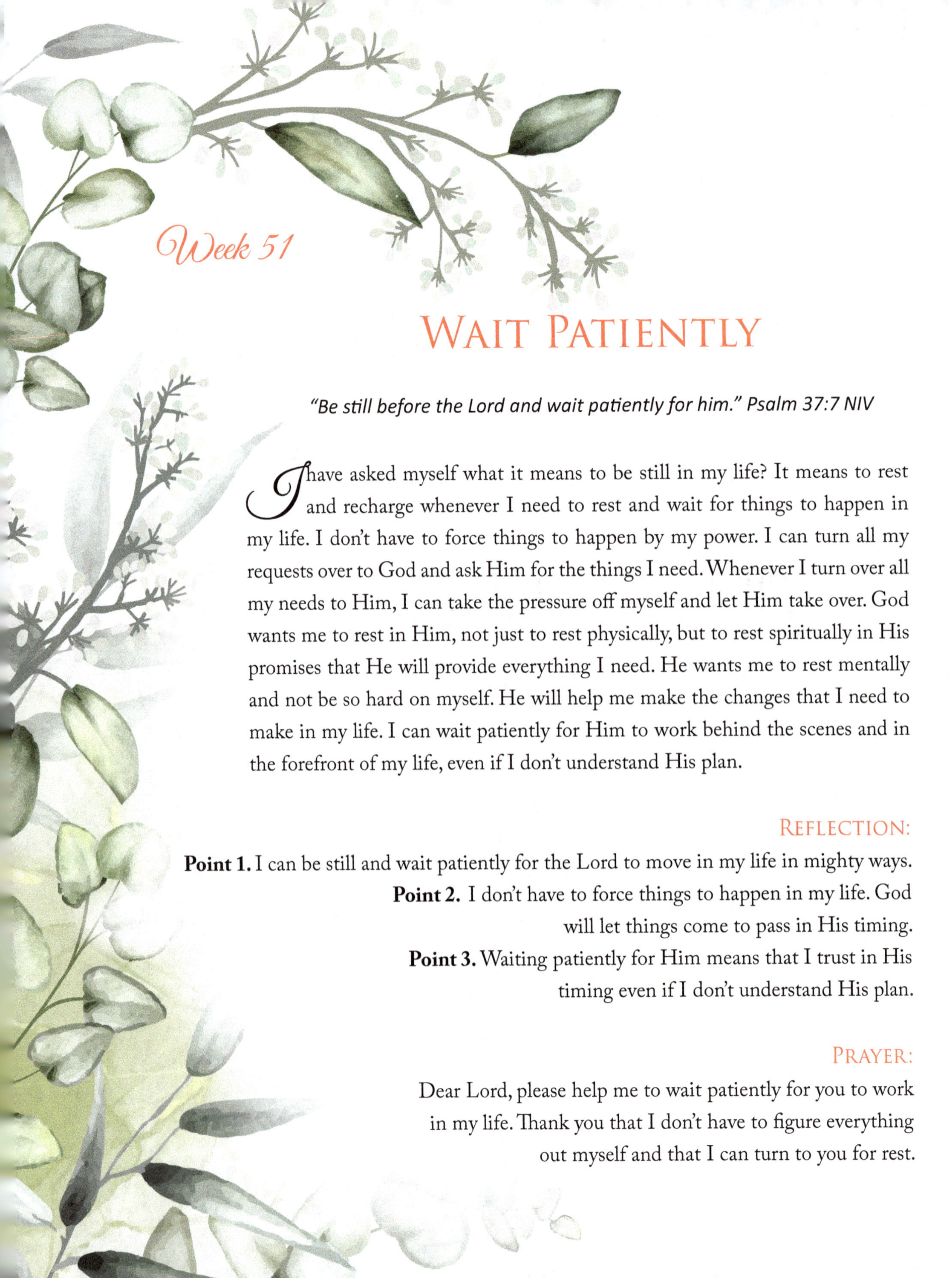

WAIT PATIENTLY

"Be still before the Lord and wait patiently for him." Psalm 37:7 NIV

I have asked myself what it means to be still in my life? It means to rest and recharge whenever I need to rest and wait for things to happen in my life. I don't have to force things to happen by my power. I can turn all my requests over to God and ask Him for the things I need. Whenever I turn over all my needs to Him, I can take the pressure off myself and let Him take over. God wants me to rest in Him, not just to rest physically, but to rest spiritually in His promises that He will provide everything I need. He wants me to rest mentally and not be so hard on myself. He will help me make the changes that I need to make in my life. I can wait patiently for Him to work behind the scenes and in the forefront of my life, even if I don't understand His plan.

REFLECTION:

Point 1. I can be still and wait patiently for the Lord to move in my life in mighty ways.

Point 2. I don't have to force things to happen in my life. God will let things come to pass in His timing.

Point 3. Waiting patiently for Him means that I trust in His timing even if I don't understand His plan.

PRAYER:

Dear Lord, please help me to wait patiently for you to work in my life. Thank you that I don't have to figure everything out myself and that I can turn to you for rest.

"Looking to Jesus, the founder and perfecter of our faith..." Hebrews 12:2

THINGS ON MY MIND

PRAYER REQUEST

PRAYERS ANSWERED

THINK ABOUT SUCH THINGS

"Finally, brothers, whatever is true, whatever is honorable, whatever is just, whatever is pure, whatever is lovely, whatever is commendable, if there is any excellence, if there is anything worthy of praise, think about these things." Philippians 4:8 NIV

When I think about everything I've gone through, I can carry the hope of Jesus in my heart. I can walk around with a different and special kind of confidence. I can have an attitude of gratitude about the way things are going. I can think about what's true. I know that Jesus died on the cross for me and that He loves me with unconditional love. I can think about what is honorable by speaking kindness over someone else, whether at work, school, or home. I can stand up for someone who can't stand up for themselves. I can think about how lovely it is to have God in my life. I can keep myself pure. I can commend someone for something nice they've done, and I can think about how amazing and excellent God is. He is worthy of being praised every single second of the day. I can think about these things every day.

REFLECTION:

Point 1. I can think about how amazing God has been throughout my life

Point 2. I can praise Him for everything and enjoy the life God has given me

Point 3. I can think about anything that is excellent and praiseworthy, and thanks to God for it.

PRAYER:

Dear Lord, please help me to think about the appropriate things in my life. Help me to stay focused on you.

"His divine power has granted to us all things that pertain to life and godliness..." 2 Peter 1:3

THINGS ON MY MIND

PRAYER REQUEST

PRAYERS ANSWERED